Nice Girls ON TOP

NICE GIRLS ON TOP

*Compassionate and Highly
Effective Leadership for Women*

Patricia Forrester

HEEKIN PRESS

Los Angeles

Published by Heekin Press, Los Angeles, California.

Cover Design: Hutchinson Design Studio
          www.hutchinsondesignstudio.com

Printed in the United States of America

ISBN: 978-0-615-42659-4

For all of us who strive to become
better people every day.

ACKNOWLEDGMENTS

My name may be the only one on the cover of this book, but it was clearly a collaborative effort. For that reason, I am so grateful to the women whose names appear within it. They so selflessly shared their time and wisdom to make this book what it is. They are the true stars!

I am extremely indebted to my editor, Matthew Hutchison. His creative insight and input enhanced this book beyond its original conception. I would also like to thank Susan Corbin Blume for her copy editing expertise and dedication.

Finally, I appreciate my family and friends for their constant support and encouragement during this entire project.

CONTENTS

FOREWORD

Nice Girls On Top. You have to admit it's a compelling title. And I must say an idea whose time has come—women winning at work by leading with compassion. It is a belief that I have held to strongly throughout my twenty-year career as an international speaker, transformational coach and change consultant. During that time, I have had the honor of helping thousands of people with their leadership styles. On and off the platform, coaching male and female executives from all over the world, including several Fortune 500 companies, I have seen firsthand that it is the collaborative, compassionate style that gets things done. Having used both styles myself, the "do it my way" and the more collaborative, I can tell you that the leader who inspires people from the very best parts of themselves, who uses kindness instead of punishment, will always be the person who is respected, followed and profitable. People want to be on a team that wins *and* where they feel valued. That empowerment and inspiration stems from working with a leader who uses compassion and collaboration to bring out the best in everyone around them. We strive to be and do more in the presence of that kind of leader. The opposite is true when fear and intimidation are present. We work in a place of fear, doing just enough to keep our jobs with a "punch the time clock" mentality. In such an environment, there is a lack of innovation and new ideas, which leads to flat-lining profits.

As women, many of us can relate to the solitary feeling of being the only woman on the team, the only woman leading, or just "that woman." It is a story we all share. What Patricia Forrester has done is take five successful women from a variety of backgrounds and pull from them the heart of what leading with compassion has won for them.

That is where the title leads us, to a change—a change in our thought processes and hopefully our hearts, which will inspire us to the inner change, belief, and fire that is so evident in the words of these women. What you will find on these pages is a compelling cause, an interpersonal insight into information and passion from these women's lives woven seamlessly into a guidebook. The following pages are an empowerment tool for women just beginning their leadership careers, those who are not yet leaders, and those well-seasoned professionals who are called to a higher place of purpose, realizing that the old top down management by intimidation and fear is not worth the costs.

Once you enter into this journey, you will exit changed. You have to. There is no other option but to leave this experience with more hope about your own intrinsic style and a passion to inspire trust, empower people, and serve others in a fearless way. You will be moved by this intimate sharing of challenges overcome, daily examples of what it takes to lead, and how to move forward as a powerful leader with qualities you already possess.

Join Ms. Forrester as she takes you on a journey with these amazing women to uncover the yet unwritten story inside yourself. It is an experience that will change you and one you won't soon forget.

Dawn Brackett
Inspirational Speaker and Coach
Leadership and Self Improvement
www.dawnbrackett.com
July, 2010

INTRODUCTION

I chose the title of this book because it counteracts any notion that "nice" girls or women cannot succeed in business. Other books will tell you differently, but I believe, and studies show, that being compassionate is actually a key ingredient to being a highly effective leader.[1] By fostering team spirit and empowering others to do their best, you can move your company to the top and have fun doing it!

The methods a leader uses to bring about an effective performance from an individual or a team can vary greatly. Some leaders use fear and intimidation to get results while others adopt a hands-off approach, believing that it is up to individuals to "sink or swim" in a competitive society. However, using compassion to inspire and lead is not only the right thing to do, it is also the most effective means of getting positive results from a team and each team member.

As mothers and nurturers, women have an instinct for compassionate and supportive leadership. Studies show that female leaders often bring new perspectives to companies and lead teams that thrive on mutual support and collaboration rather than a top down patriarchy. Such a refreshing leadership approach has been adopted by many companies in this new information age we live in and actually works better than the old dictatorial methods.[2]

Being nice (i.e., compassionate, kind, nurturing, etc.) may come more naturally to women, but these traits are not exclusive to women. Many men in business have succeeded by employing the kind and compassionate methods described in this book. Still, this book is primarily aimed at women who are discouraged from following their natural nurturing instincts in a misguided attempt to succeed in the same manner that men frequently have in the past. As the evidence in this book shows, there is no need for women in leadership to feel that they have to choose between being nice and being effective, because one leads to the other.

Unfortunately, though, women have been getting mixed signals for years. First, women were told that they had to "act like men" in order to succeed. But women who assert themselves are often unfairly criticized.

If women are approaching the task of leadership with confusion today, it is no wonder. For many years, women rarely had the opportunity to move to the top of any company. Many of the women who did break through, though, felt that they had to act in a brutish manner and play along with the fear-based patriarchy of male-dominated leadership. For me, personally, that was a big disappointment. I saw a lot of women going against their better nature and didn't feel I could look up to them. I was looking for female role models and was saddened when these women in high places acted in this manner.

I can understand why some women in leadership have tended to act like brutes, though. Like me, they were looking for female role models and did not see many, if any, in the business world. So, in turn, these women emulated the stereotype of what was considered the successful male boss, someone who was usually ego-driven and commanded others to do his bidding. Adding strength to this tendency for many years was the belief that being nice and being a woman was a losing combination in business. Women, in general, were viewed as too soft or weak to be part of the tough "survivor of the fittest" male-dominated business world. Many female leaders who were lucky enough to move up the ladder in business felt that they had to act as tough and intimidating as their male counterparts in order to break down doors and crack the glass ceilings.

Where does such bad treatment of each other find its roots? For years, many businesses and corporations were set up as hierarchies and were led by fear. This model dates back to the industrial age where the machine was valued more than the person.[3] In the industrial age, management modeled their industries after the military.[4] Of course, the military is not the workplace, so that was never the right fit. Military leadership involves depersonalizing people. The reason for this is that soldiers are going "as a unit" into situations where they may be killed. Individual ideas in this case can be dangerous. When the industrial age came along, companies took the military's hierarchical system and applied it to people on the assembly lines. Managers would walk down the line, yelling and keeping everyone on task, and the corporate structure started expanding above that. Even today, in many corporations, employees are made to feel that their feelings and opinions do not matter. They are part of a machine, so they should just do their jobs and keep their mouths shut.

We no longer live in the industrial age, but rather in the information age where people and individual ideas should be valued. Companies like the highly successful Google, Dreamworks Animation SKG, and J.M. Smucker realize this fact, as shown in a February 2010 *Fortune* magazine study.[5] Under their management styles, employees are free to exhibit their individual talents more often and to explore new ideas. Employees are increasingly treated with kindness and respect, creating an atmosphere in which they are more likely to do their best. People are not being micromanaged to such an extreme that they are always in fear of making mistakes or, even worse, losing their jobs. In turn, the best and the brightest people want to work for companies that implement such a management style.

Not only is the new management model of being kind and respecting employees being touted more and more, but scientific studies have demonstrated that if you treat your employees with kindness and respect, you will get better performance.[6]

Still, many companies are stuck in the past when it comes to their treatment of employees, not realizing that the old way of leading by fear actually leads to many unwanted results, such as stress-related illnesses, lowered employee performance, and negative views of employers by employees.[7] It is true that many companies have human resources departments that protect people's civil rights, but being kind or compassionate is still not viewed as a requirement. Being "nice" is still considered by many in the business world to be a weakness, as if your employees will walk all over you if you show them any kindness.

Because of that, women are still getting mixed signals. Women hear, "Be yourselves, but be tough like men." Books are still being printed with titles that begin with "Nice Girls Don't Get..." The basic message that both men and women still get is that, in terms of business, it does not pay to be nice.

According to the information age management model, it pays really well to be nice! As the aforementioned *Fortune* magazine study demonstrates, companies that employ compassionate business practices are some of the most profitable companies in America today.

In terms of leadership, what is the proper definition of "nice"? As used herein, it simply means to act as a compassionate guide or mentor who inspires and empowers others to do their best. Being "nice" does not mean being a pushover, though, nor does it mean accepting less than the best results possible. As this book demonstrates, highly effective team leaders are often the most compassionate as well.

Panel of Experts

For this book, I interviewed five women. Each of them was chosen not only because she is highly successful in her field as a leader, but also because she is universally regarded by her employees and co-workers as being fair and compassionate. Being "nice" is not merely a moral choice; all of these women know that it makes them successful leaders, and it does. In the following chapters, we hear specifically how these leaders, who are demonstrably both compassionate (or "nice") *and* effective, meet the common challenges that arise in leading a successful company or enterprise. We also get to hear their insights into how they developed their compassionate leadership styles and who inspired them to believe that positive results can best be achieved through such positive leadership techniques. They have made a choice to be good role models and have not allowed themselves to take the "low road" to becoming successful at the expense of others. In this book, they offer guidance about how to lead in a kind and compassionate manner *and* be successful.

I have designed this book to simulate a transcript of a women's panel on compassionate and highly effective leadership. In this simulated panel discussion taken from the interviews, I ask the questions and the panel answers, giving valuable information for anyone who wants to brush up on their leadership skills. You may notice some repetition in what people are saying, but it only proves the point that certain techniques work and are implemented by the best leaders.

This book is divided into three parts. In the first part, I ask questions about the development of the interviewees' leadership skills. These women learned in different ways: by learning from their own families, by taking advantage of opportunities in school, by volunteering, by being mothers, and by learning from role models and mentors. The purpose of this section is to let you, the reader, know that you may have learned or are still learning such leadership skills in your everyday interactions. You may or may not have had the ideal family or school experience. Maybe you cannot even think of a good leadership role model in your life, but upon reflection, you may find that you have learned compassionate and effective leadership skills in some of these circumstances nonetheless.

The second part deals with leading a team or staff in a compassionate and highly effective manner. Again, I ask the panel questions, and the panel gives answers that will help guide you if you are new to leadership, if you would like to improve your skills, or if you simply need a reminder of good leadership methods. This section can serve as a "go to" guide whenever you find yourself in a predicament with your staff.

Finally, the third part deals with advantages and disadvantages of being a woman in a leadership role at work. The panel shares their views about how being a woman can help or hinder in a work environment that still may be confusing for many female leaders.

So, without further ado, I would like to introduce you to this wonderful panel...five nice girls who are definitely on top!

Jennifer O'Connell

Jennifer O'Connell is Executive Vice President of the television production company Shed Media US. In her capacity, Jennifer serves not only as an executive developing shows, but also serves as Executive Producer of many of the company's successful television shows, which include NBC's *Who Do You Think You Are?*, Bravo's *The Real Housewives of New York City*, and Bravo's *Bethenny Getting Married.* Jennifer also served as an Executive Producer on NBC's *The Marriage Ref* (created by Jerry Seinfeld).

Previously, Jennifer served several years as an executive at NBC as Vice President of Alternative Programming (reality shows) as well as Vice President of Movies, where she oversaw the development of such hit programs as *The Biggest Loser* and the Emmy Award-winning *The Matthew Shepard Story*.

A sixteen-year veteran of the television industry, Jennifer also served as a creative executive at both the Disney Channel and Family Channel. In addition, Jennifer is a member of the Academy of Television Arts and Sciences and the Caucus for Producers, Writers & Directors.

Jennifer received a bachelor's degree in speech communications from Emerson College in Boston, Massachusetts.

Elizabeth Amini

Elizabeth Amini is the CEO of Anti-AgingGames.com, which features games scientifically designed to stimulate brain function. These memory and focus games were designed by a panel of expert neurobehavioral scientists in collaboration with Nolan Bushnell, the Founder of Atari and Chuck E. Cheese. The Anti-AgingGames system also gives tips on how to reduce the risk of early memory loss. The games are fun and easy and designed for people over 35.

Elizabeth's Anti-Aging Games business plan won the USC Business Plan contest as well as the YPO (Young Presidents' Organization) award for promising new companies. While many of her company's competitors focus on nursing and retirement homes, Anti-

AgingGames.com targets people who are one or two generations younger because, they reason, brain fitness programs are more effective if training starts earlier.

Before receiving her master's degree in business at the University of Southern California (USC), Elizabeth graduated with a bachelor's degree in cognitive science (the study of the brain) with a focus on pre-medicine from Occidental College in Los Angeles. Realizing she didn't want to become a doctor, Elizabeth tried various careers, including running her own graphic design company, leading a research study at JPL/NASA, heading up her own business consulting firm, and being a strategy consultant at one of the top management consulting firms in the world.

Social responsibility is very important to Elizabeth. Anti-AgingGames.com donates 20% of its pre-tax profits to improve lives around the world, including taking medicine, supplies, and clean water access to refugee camps, disaster areas, and poverty-stricken areas around the world through carefully screened nonprofit partners.

Alma Robinson

Alma Robinson has been the Executive Director of California Lawyers for the Arts (C.L.A.) for nearly 30 years. This non-profit organization, with three offices in California, establishes a bridge between the arts and legal communities so that artists and art groups may gain greater competence in handling the legal and business aspects of their creative activities.

Alma has many career achievements that include: developing a seven-agency collaboration providing cultural enrichment activities for 5,000 San Francisco youth (Culture Core), developing a national mediation network (Arts Resolution Services) with collaborating art/law organizations in Houston, New York City, Chicago, Denver, St. Louis and Washington, D.C., and developing a technical assistance program focused on opportunities for the arts at converted military bases with support from the NEA (National Endowment for the Arts) Design Arts Program.

Alma is the recipient of many awards and honors, including the California Arts Council Director's Award for Outstanding Leadership as well as the Women's Caucus for Art (Northern CA Region) Lifetime Achievement Award.

Alma received a bachelor's degree in history from Middlebury College in Vermont and a juris doctor degree from Stanford University Law School.

Melanie Merians

Melanie Merians has two occupations, both in the non-profit arena. After five years of working for Girl Scouts of Greater Los Angeles, Melanie recently moved on to become the Chief Development and Communications Officer for Covenant House California, a statewide agency serving homeless and at-risk youth. Melanie also works in a voluntary capacity as the U.S. Western Territory Women's Leader of the Soka Gakkai International-USA (SGI-USA), a Buddhist lay organization committed to peace, culture, and education.

Melanie's business leadership style is informed by her Buddhist practice which acknowledges the vast and respect-worthy potential of all. Instead of a typical corporate hierarchy, she prefers to build trust by creating an effective matrix-style system where teams interface, experience tremendous synergy, and accomplish set goals.

In her position with the SGI-USA, Melanie inspires others in the practice of Buddhism by giving motivational speeches, leading meetings, and encouraging individuals to use the humanistic principles of Buddhism to challenge themselves to become better people and lead contributive lives.

Melanie received a bachelor's degree in theater at Vassar College in New York, a certificate in filmmaking at New York University, and spent several years as an executive working in international and domestic film distribution.

Note: At the time of this interview, Melanie was still working at the Girl Scouts of Greater Los Angeles in an executive capacity.

Lane Jensen

Lane Jensen has had a variety of careers, starting as an owner of a chain of restaurants and then as producer and executive producer in the advertising and entertainment industries. She is currently working as the Vice President of Operations for Frameworks Music.

During Lane's career, she produced the Emmy Award winning main titles for the show *Six Feet Under*, the Emmy Award nominated titles for *Desperate Housewives*, and numerous other main titles and television commercials while working with the nationally recognized motion graphics firms yU+Co and Digital Kitchen. She has worked with ad agencies, television networks, corporations, and film production companies such as Columbia Pictures, MGM, Fox, HBO, CBS, DDB, Euro RSCG Paris among others. Lane is highly skilled in overseeing productions and creating an atmosphere for the creative to excel.

Lane attended the Kansas City Art Institute and graduated from the University of Washington with a bachelor's degree in art.

PART I

BECOMING A LEADER

CHAPTER 1

Lessons Learned in the Family

We may not be aware of it, but we learn a lot about leadership from our families. We watch our parents and see them take charge of situations. They may not be perfect role models, but we observe leadership traits in them that may turn out to be beneficial or that we may adopt later. Family dynamics and our position in the family (sibling order) may have an influence on our leadership style as well. I asked the panel what they learned about leadership from their family situations and here are the answers they gave…

Do you think you learned anything about leadership in your family? For example, what did you learn from your parents? Did your placement in the family (first, middle, youngest, or only) have an impact at all?

Jennifer

Both of my parents are good role models. My Mom was the oldest of five children, and she was always the one that planned everything. Growing up, I remember, all the big holidays were at our house, and she was always in charge and in control. My Dad started his own business and is now partnered with my Mom. That has always inspired me, to see someone take that risk and do their own thing. I haven't started my own company, but I definitely took a risk when I left the network to work in production. So, I feel I took on my Dad's entrepreneurial spirit.

Being the firstborn in my family like my Mom, I did everything first. There's a pressure to succeed, and there's a pressure to be the leader of your siblings. I have a younger sister and two younger brothers, and I have a desire to take care of them, but I think it comes with the older sister territory. I would say that I'm definitely an outspoken leader in the family, too, much to some of my family members' chagrin. As a kid, I didn't consider being the oldest sibling as a leadership role. As I've gotten older, I look back and realize that it actually was.

Lane

I am the oldest child in the family, so naturally I took a leadership role. It is not even something that your parents put on you as much as you put on yourself. You feel responsible because you have younger brothers and sisters and you care about them and want things to go well for all of you, so you do tend to be a little bit of the ringleader. You think, "These are my people and I need to protect them." My parents would even say, "Oh, Lane is very mature for her age. Lane does this. Lane does that," which made me view myself as somebody that accepted responsibility. Because of my role in the family, it became just natural for me to assume leadership positions throughout my life.

I would also add that my parents allowed and empowered me to be a leader. They saw my potential and nudged me into leadership positions whenever the opportunity arose. My Mom always had confidence in me. She thought that I could handle situations and that I would thrive if given responsibility.

Both of my parents had integrity and a good work ethic, which they passed on to me, but they also steered me towards art. My Mom loved museums, and the first thing we would do when we got to a new town was to go see the art museum. I think that not only contributed to my appreciation of art, but helped me develop my "artistic eye," which has helped me tremendously in my career.

Elizabeth

I'm the oldest child, and I have a younger sister. I definitely watched over my younger sister while we were growing up, but I think we were and still are an entire family of leaders. My parents encouraged that. They didn't ask for obedience too much. I think when you ask a kid to do things and you say, "Because I said so," and you don't give a real answer, then the kid learns to follow. Whereas in our house, when I did something wrong, they would say, "What do you think your punishment should be?" I would gauge my own punishment, and, oddly enough, I would deal it out fairly. Also, watching them in action helped. My parents were great role models. They are both doctors and I remember whenever there was an earthquake, they would spend a lot of time buying medicine and repackaging it. For example, they would buy a lot of bottles of Tylenol, dump out the pills and compress them into one bottle so that it was really full. They would then ship the medicine over to the place that had the earthquake. Just seeing them spring into action and help whenever they could made a lasting impression on me.

Melanie

I had a great example in both my parents. My father was a very creative businessman who had a tremendous sense of integrity and decency and was always very well respected and admired by the people who worked for him. In that sense, he was a good role model. My mother was also a fine role model for her kindness and emotional support. She also had her own strong values and lived by them and didn't mind what others thought.

I'm the middle child with one older and one younger sister. My older sister was a businesswoman and my younger sister was an artist up until fairly recently. I am in between "the artist" and "the business person." My mother saw herself more as an artist, and my father obviously *was* a businessman. Growing up, I sometimes felt outside the family dynamic. I had my own tendencies, my own darkness, and my own negativity, which pulled me to the outside of the family. At a young age, for many emotional reasons, I sought to be independent. I started earning my own money, and it gave me a sense of freedom and empowerment that I didn't need to ask my father for money, even though my family was well off and certainly had money. I babysat and did odd jobs. I worked during the summers, even when I was a young girl. It was very clear that I wanted to be able to make my own choices, have my own path, earn my own money and have my own life. Because of my sense of independence from the family, I tended to always be seen as a leader of whatever social group I was in when I was young, which is interesting.

Alma

One of my earliest memories was being really scared by a large dog growling at us when I was walking home with my brother and my mother. My brother, Carlton, who was a year younger than me, took my hand and said, "Don't worry little sister, don't be afraid." Carlton died of a mysterious illness when he was two years old and I was three, so I grew up as an only child. As a result of my brother's death, and my own near brush at the age of five after a tonsillectomy, my parents were very protective of me. But they always made sure that I had opportunities to participate in all kinds of enrichment activities, such as piano lessons, school orchestra and choruses, summer camps,

Girl Scouts, Advanced Placement History at a high school across town, and so forth.

Being an only child, I got to experience a lot of the best things our town had to offer with my parents, one-on-one. My mother, Gladys Mauney Robinson, took me to see Leontyne Price, the great opera singer, when she came to perform at Winston-Salem Teachers College, my mother's alma mater (now Winston-Salem State University). My father, Willie, or Robbie, as my mother called him, took me to baseball games—making me a lifelong fan—and to hear Martin Luther King at a Baptist Church in our neighborhood. But when I was in high school, they refused to let me go to the 1963 March on Washington. They thought it was too dangerous.

My mother was a first grade teacher. According to a cousin, Jimmie Franklin, there were over 90 teachers in our family, including my grandmother, Isabel, and my mother's sisters, Ruth and Agnes. Teaching was one of the few professions available to black people back then. I used to help my mother with the bulletin boards in her classrooms prior to the start of the school year. No doubt, that was my first volunteer experience and I assumed that, if all else failed, I could become a teacher. We all had "teaching genes."

Both of my parents were great models for "the work ethic." My mother was very committed to her students, often beyond the classroom. If "her kids" had problems, she would help them with whatever they needed, even pulling loose teeth! My father was a machinist at a tobacco factory, and also a very hard worker, not only there, but also in the community. After he retired, he was really active in our church, where they called him "the lead man." He also loved helping neighbors up and down the street. If anyone needed anything, he was the go-to guy. He never minded going the extra mile.

They both had lots of friends and were very engaged with our extended families. Every summer, we'd drive down to Gaston County, near Charlotte, for the Mauney family reunion, an annual tradition started by my great-grandfather and two of his cousins in 1906. Over and over, we learned the family history, all the way back to Guinea in West Africa. Through regular visits back and forth, my relationships with my cousins took the place of the siblings I didn't have, and I'm still close to many of them.

I also remember that it was so annoying to go anywhere in town with my parents, because they knew everybody and would stop everywhere and talk to people endlessly. Looking back, I think this taught me a lot about social interaction and the importance of taking the time to stop and be present with people. If you listen long enough, even if you think you've heard the story before, you can often find a gem of wisdom or humor or just plain common sense.

Once in a while, I'd get to be the leader in the family, or so I thought. For example, when we went on vacation, I was the one who would unfold the map, find directions, and give instructions to the driver. I remember feeling good that my parents could rely on me to find our way in unfamiliar places. What this taught me about leadership was that you don't always have to be the one in charge who knows all the answers. You can give others the tools and delegate some of the responsibility to them. Let them sort out the problems, apply the resources, and come up with the solutions. Then you have the foundation of a team rather than a hierarchy.

Lessons from Parents

Our first encounter with leadership is seeing our parents take charge of different situations. Although most parents are not perfect, they teach us a lot. The women in this book were influenced—and so is everyone, for better or worse—by their parents. Luckily, these women had the experience of learning many compassionate and constructive qualities from their parents.

Several panelists mention that the most effective teaching method used by their parents was role modeling rather than verbal instruction. By witnessing the behaviors of their parents, the panelists gleaned appropriate behaviors and values that would later come to serve them as leaders. Melanie witnessed her father being a decent man with integrity, which demonstrated to her strength of character. Jennifer saw her mother take charge of situations and her father take risks, which made her feel that she, too, could attempt those kinds of actions. Lane's parents taught her the importance of raising the next generation of leaders. They did this by encouraging Lane to take responsibility and leadership positions when available. They also showed her that a good leader empowers and inspires others.

In each of these cases, though, probably the most valuable lesson taught to the panelists was the importance of role modeling, in itself. No one will listen to someone who is unable to live by what he or she says. For example, if a leader says, "Do the best job possible," and always does a sloppy job, then he or she will be not be effective. A good leader always leads the way first so others will understand and follow. By role modeling great leadership qualities, the panelists' parents were being highly effective. Showing people how to do things, rather than just telling them, is compassionate as well.

In terms of compassion, most panelists spoke of how their parents demonstrated kindness. For example, both Alma and Elizabeth saw the importance of helping others: Alma's mother would go the extra mile for her students and her father was the neighborhood go-to guy, while Elizabeth's parents sprang into action to help disaster victims. Melanie, too, saw how her mother offered kindness and emotional support to others when needed.

Ideally, parenting is a wonderful example of compassionate leadership because most parents love their children and have their best interests at heart. What if business leaders acted more like parents? The business world can never and should not imitate a family model completely, but leadership methods learned from parents can still be instructive and inspiring.

One may wonder if there is any hope for people with bad parents. One possibility is for a child of poor parenting to learn through "counter-example"—that is, seeing a parent's behavior as "what <u>not</u> to do," although this is a tougher lesson to learn. Another possibility is to find role models in people other than one's parents, especially in cases where parents are absent or ineffective. Many happy and successful people have found valuable nurturing from siblings, teachers, counselors or more distant relatives, for example.

Sibling Order

Another question I asked the panel was about their position in the family and how that may have affected their leadership style. The ones who were the oldest definitely felt a responsibility to take the lead, but others developed their own perspective and sense of independence.

As the oldest of their siblings, Lane and Jennifer feel that they were indeed leaders in the family. They felt the responsibilities of taking care of their younger brothers and sisters. It wasn't just expected, but there was a want and need to watch over their younger siblings. Jennifer also felt a bit of pressure to succeed and do everything first. So, consciously or unconsciously, she was acting as a role model to her younger siblings by taking risks and showing her sister and brothers how to behave as well. Elizabeth, too, is the oldest sibling. She feels, though, that both she and her younger sister were encouraged to be leaders in their own right. Most of that leadership training, she believes, came from watching her parents in their actions and behavior.

Alma and Melanie had different family dynamics. For Melanie, as the middle child, she felt like a bit of an outsider. She may not have gotten the focus of her older and younger sisters, but it did push her to be more of an independent spirit. Being an only child, Alma saw another perspective and was influenced more by the role modeling behavior of her parents. As an only child, she also received more attention from her parents and was encouraged to succeed. She was also offered many opportunities that would otherwise have been divided among other siblings.

Family – Our First Team

Another lesson learned in the family is teamwork. Ideally, the family we are born into is a group of people who support and encourage each other in the most compassionate way possible. In this best case scenario, the family is everyone's first exposure to teamwork. Parents are naturally the leaders, but they teach their children through trial and error how each member of the family should support each other. Each member can rely on the other members for guidance and protection from a sometimes cruel and stressful world. Alma's example of her extended family shows, too, how a family and all its connections can empower an individual through a common bond that links back to earlier generations. Knowing her family history, Alma developed a sense of pride that shows in the telling of her family's story. Her extended family also gave Alma a sense of mission and pride, for example by knowing that her family had the "teaching" gene.

Although everyone in our panel had positive family experiences, not everyone is so lucky. One may not have had the fortune to be born in a healthy family or to be aware of one's own ancestry. Hopefully, though, such an individual will find other ways to be exposed to a different kind of family—not necessarily related, but a group of people who are bonded and committed to one another for a greater good. This kind of family is often referred to as a "family of choice." Such a family can not only take the place of a traditional family, but can be the model for a leader to learn how to work with a team and understand how to lead that team with compassion and collaboration.

In conclusion, our family situation not only has a lot to do with how we approach life, but also how we approach leadership. For better or worse, our parents are our role models. Ideally, our parents will possess good leadership traits, which we will then adopt. Even less-than-effective or unloving parents can provide occasional positive examples or, in the worst cases, examples of behaviors to avoid. In a broader sense, our family will also teach us how a team works together in a compassionate and collaborative manner. Finally, our family dynamic has great influence on us. As the women on the panel demonstrate, being the oldest may seem like an advantage when it comes to leadership, but no matter where one is positioned in the family, one can develop her (or his) own leadership style.

CHAPTER 2

Lessons Learned in School

We start learning a lot about leadership during our school years. Not everyone gets involved in student government or other organizations, but many of us develop an independent spirit and take advantage of opportunities in school to develop leadership qualities. I asked the panel to reflect back to their high school and college years and, after some reflection, each was able to recognize some kind of potential she was developing.

How did you develop your leadership skills during your school years?

Jennifer

In high school (in Connecticut), I decided that I wanted to be involved in the local access television station. I figured out who was in charge of it, and I went to them and said, "I want to do the East Hartford High School News." I made my best friend do it with me because I wanted a partner in crime. As that evolved, the local movie theater wanted us to review movies, so we did that. I really liked the behind-the-scenes part of making the show, and, even then, I knew I wanted to be involved in the television industry.

That's what led me to Emerson College in Boston. I was always thinking three steps ahead; I knew that Emerson had a program for television in Los Angeles where most students do their senior year. I knew that if I wanted to be in the television industry, I should live in Los Angeles. Emerson has everything you need if you want to be in the television industry, but it's up to you to be proactive.

In my initial years at Emerson, I joined different campus organizations, such as the campus radio station, WERS, and the school's television station. I worked on shows there right from the start. I also joined a sorority to make new friends. In all of these situations, I would take roles where I would be part of the leadership circle, so my ideas could be heard and maybe implemented.

My ultimate goal, though, was to have internships, to be exposed to the television industry, and then to hopefully turn all of that into a job. My first two internships were in the public relations field in Boston. Finally, in my senior year, I came out to Los Angeles and did an internship at Paramount Studios in the Public Relations Department. Then, the Head of Television's assistant wanted an intern and, even though I didn't get paid, I took the position. It was an incredible opportunity, and I wanted to take advantage of it. I had my own little intern office with a nice window looking out on the Paramount lot. It was a very calm office with high profile people coming in and out. I learned a lot by just observing what was happening in that office. It was Garry Hart's office, who used to run Paramount Television Studios. Years later, my husband ended up working for Garry, which is a funny coincidence. I don't know how I knew it, but I guess I knew that the more exposure I had, the better off I'd be. If it wasn't in media, somewhere down the line, it wouldn't hurt to have met these people.

Elizabeth

My first leadership position was actually working on the school newspaper in high school. I was managing others and putting together sections of the newspaper at that time. Things weren't computerized, so we were actually printing things out, sticking them on the page with hot wax and building the pages physically to be run off by the newspaper. It was the kind of job where there were such strong deadlines, and there was so much to be done, that you just rolled up your sleeves and did it. Some of the work was delegated out to others, but, for the most part, we really had to stay up late and just get it done. We didn't have too many meetings, but everybody was dedicated and came together.

I worked on the school newspaper when I got to college at Occidental too. Friday mornings were the deadlines and almost every Thursday night everybody would stay up all night and work on the paper. The first year in college, I was in charge of all of the advertising; the second year, I became a co-editor for sections of the newspaper. We had to manage a lot of people—the ad sales people, the writers, and the graphic designers. I learned a lot then.

In college, I also started the school's sailing club and became its president as well as volunteering as a peer mentor. I ended up learning a lot from the mentees. Sometimes, it was kind of hard to tell who the mentor was and who the mentee was because everyone comes with knowledge.

Lane

I went to college in Kansas City, at the Kansas City Art Institute. It was a small school with about 1,200 kids. They didn't really have a standard college student body government. It was the kind of school where they would buy a keg on weekends so we could all party. It was a very different environment than a university setting. We were very hard working with our art projects and with academics. I was always an over-achiever. Later on, I went back to college in Seattle and took business classes. While there, I volunteered to be a peer advisor helping other students sign up for classes. I acted as a counselor by listening and helping students decide what courses to take. I loved that experience. I just knew then that not only did I really like helping others excel, but it felt very natural for me to have that role with people.

Melanie

I went to Vassar for undergraduate school. I earned a degree in theater with a minor in English. Then I went to New York University for a filmmaking program. At Vassar, there was a lot of work involved outside of class with theater—rehearsals, costumes, backstage work, and set building. I starred in productions and directed plays as well. That process of working with others and directing helped in the development of my leadership skills. Having said that, though, I saw myself as kind of an outsider. I was trying to graduate early and took a heavy course load at Columbia over the summers. I went in with one class and I graduated with another. My social skills were very under-developed, too, because I went to school when I was young and graduated by the time I was 20.

Alma

Anderson High School in Winston-Salem, North Carolina was a segregated school that had meager course offerings and few leadership opportunities. Of course, there were no sports for girls back in the 1960's; instead, I was drawn to theatre and music for extracurricular activities. I also worked on the school yearbook and became a high school correspondent for our afternoon newspaper, the Winston-Salem Sentinel. My parents encouraged me to go past my comfort zone when I was accepted into certain honors programs, like the statewide

Governor's School for high school students at Salem College, and an advanced placement history course taught at Reynolds, a large white high school across town. When the history teacher told us that I couldn't share a hotel room with any of the white girls during a class trip to New York City, my parents paid the fee for my classmate from Anderson so that she could accompany me. During the trip North, the white students kindly brought food to us as we waited on the bus after it stopped at a roadside restaurant for dinner. It was a difficult time.

During my college years at Middlebury, I continued to write for the school newspaper and spent two summers working at the Winston-Salem Journal and Sentinel. Across the country, black students were participating in the Civil Rights Movement. Even in our sublime isolation in Vermont, our small group of African-American students at Middlebury took a stand for greater diversity. I was one of two students who negotiated with the Dean of Students, who successfully pre-empted our planned "takeover" of administrative offices by coming to us first to ask us what we wanted.

Later, when I went to Stanford Law School, I became active in student government and raised funds for various projects. That is where I hit my stride in terms of leadership. During my second year, I helped organize a special orientation for incoming minority students in the next class. We wanted to help the new people get on board and feel comfortable with the situation at Stanford. I think that effort really made a difference by building their confidence and helping them succeed.

In my third year, I volunteered as the yearbook editor and photographer, which gave me an opportunity to get to know many of my classmates really well. I was also elected vice-president of the class. I did not aspire to be a leader, but rather, I evolved. I stepped up to the plate and followed the opportunities and responded to the challenges that were in front of me.

The women on the panel learned many qualities of compassionate and effective leadership by taking advantage of the opportunities offered by their respective schools. For example, the panelists learned the following important lessons: 1) working with others proactively toward a goal; 2) using leadership to better communicate with and persuade others; 3) using leadership to empower oneself and others; 4) leading by being a mentor; 5) how interning can prepare for leadership; and 5) how a passion can turn into a mission to lead others.

1. Leading others toward a goal: Many on the panel participated in extracurricular activities where they led others toward a common goal. For example, Elizabeth took leadership roles for her high school and college newspapers where she managed and delegated to others. Elizabeth's recollection in both instances was that it was a team of people who were dedicated and came together to meet strong deadlines every week. There was no time for disagreement, because they had to accomplish so much in so little time, and they did. Everyone had a passion for being there, and so Elizabeth was learning to lead in a collaborative manner. In law school, Alma worked in student government and as the yearbook editor and learned many of those same skills as well. Melanie learned a lot by being involved with her theater group at Vassar. She learned to come together with a team to put on productions on a continuing basis. She also had the opportunity to exercise her leadership skills as a director in a fun and creative environment. The leadership opportunities in all of these circumstances are good ways to learn compassionate and effective leadership. Since no one is getting paid, each person has to exercise careful diplomacy, usually through trial and error, to get others to listen and follow.

*2. **Using leadership to persuade others:** Some of the panelists took on well-defined leadership roles in clubs and student government because they had ideas they believed in and used their leadership positions to persuade others. In such a scenario, a student can learn a lot about how to be diplomatic and excite others about projects. It is also a good way to learn the fine art of* *communicating and working with others, not only with fellow students, but with the school faculty as well. In Alma's situation, she was able to negotiate with faculty in order to preempt a protest and "takeover" by her fellow African-American students, who were requesting more diversity at the school. Learning how to better communicate and collaborate are definitely skills that benefit any leader.*

3. Using leadership to empower oneself and others: All of the women on the panel will attest that they experienced a great surge of self-confidence when they took on leadership roles. After all, taking the initiative to become a leader in any endeavor can be daunting, but also can be very empowering. The best example of this is when people take a stand for something, as in their rights as an individual or on behalf of a group of people. In Alma's situation, she had experienced a lot of discrimination in her youth. She didn't quit or give up, but kept going. By not giving up and taking advantage of any opportunity she could, she empowered herself. As in the case of the student demonstration at her college, she got the chance to take a stand for civil rights—that not only empowered her, but all of the students involved. This example is truly compassionate leadership!

4. How interning can prepare for leadership: Another way of taking advantage of school opportunities is by interning. As an observer, an intern gets to see how people in management behave and witness appropriate role model behavior. The preparation and training an internship provides will enhance anyone's job skills, so they will more likely behave in a secure and confident manner when given the opportunity for leadership. Jennifer had such an opportunity by observing many high profile executives at her television internship at Paramount Studios and witnessed firsthand how a leader in that position behaves. Having that internship experience proved quite beneficial to Jennifer in her later years as an executive at NBC and now as an executive producer of several television shows.

5. Leading by being a mentor: The women on the panel also learned compassionate and effective leadership in the most obvious ways by helping others. Lane became a peer advisor and found the experience very rewarding. By listening and helping students decide what courses to take, Lane discovered that helping others felt very natural for her. Working as a peer mentor, Elizabeth realized that she was learning from, as much as teaching, her mentee. Such a humbling experience is definitely great practice for compassionate and effective leadership, because all involved are learning from and teaching each other. Alma and her classmates put together a special orientation in which they helped incoming minority students become acquainted with Stanford and the law school experience. Leading while serving others is truly compassionate leadership and effective because it benefits everyone involved.

*6. **Turning a passion into leadership:** The school environment can be a wonderful opportunity for developing leadership skills in a natural and non-intimidating way by pursuing one's hobbies or interests in conjunction with others. As several panelists mention, being a leader was not a stated goal when they were students, but an organic outgrowth of working with a team. An interest in theater or television leads to involvement in a club or organization. A desire to achieve a goal then requires someone to serve as a leader. In Elizabeth's case, there was no existing organization at all, so a love of sailing required her to actually create an organization and become its leader! Likewise, Jennifer started a television news program for her school. In all these cases, leadership is not the goal but a means to an end inspired by passion and creativity.*

Such a model might serve one well in the business world. In a world where political and corporate structures already exist and are firmly entrenched, it is easy to focus on leadership as an end in itself. This behavior is ego-driven, assuming that fulfillment will come from "being President" or "being CEO." However, effective -- and thus compassionate -- leaders focus not on themselves but on a higher goal. The question should be "What can I <u>do</u> as

President?" or "What can I <u>achieve</u> as CEO?" Leadership is thus not a personal achievement but a means or a tool to achieving a common goal. How much better would our world be if political and business leaders behaved less like power-hungry hotshots and more like a group of students in love with journalism or sailing?

Finally, the purpose of this chapter is to suggest opportunities and invite reflection. If you are in college now, you may want to take advantage of these aforementioned opportunities to develop the compassionate and effective leadership skills that these women learned in their academic careers. If you are reading this book after college, you may reflect that you did indeed develop yourself in some capacity while in school, through the opportunities the school offered or by your own design. Of course, one can always return to school at any time to learn and take on leadership roles in a variety of ways that will enhance other aspects of life. But finally, the avocational spirit that we all observe in youthful or collegiate organizations can serve as an inspiring example of compassionate and effective leadership in its purest, most collaborative form, and a reminder of why we aspire to be leaders in the first place.

CHAPTER 3

Learning from Altruistic Action –
Volunteering and Parenting

Altruistic action is probably the best way to learn how to become not only a leader but a compassionate one as well. After all, when you give your time and service to others for selfless reasons, such an experience cannot help but change your perspective. The question I posed to the panel was originally about volunteer work, but I noticed that the women who were mothers would also bring up how the experience of motherhood contributed to their perspectives as well. Naturally, being a mother is probably the best leadership training a woman could possibly have.

VOLUNTEERISM

How has being a volunteer helped you become a better leader?

Elizabeth

I learned most of my leadership through volunteering. I showed up at the local Red Cross Disaster Services office when I was in my mid twenties. I had seen their ad asking for people who are bilingual to help out. I called the Red Cross and told them that I spoke other languages and asked them what they needed. They basically shoved me into a vendor partnership role, setting up all the partnerships with stores. For example, when somebody's house burns down, they don't hand them cash, but certificates instead. These certificates would be from places like Ralphs, Sizzler or a Ross clothing store. That way, people could buy clothes, get food, and go to hotels and spend the night until they had other accommodations. Upon my arrival, I told them that I had no experience whatsoever in anything corporate at that point. I was surprised when they told me, "If you have a pulse, then you are qualified to do any kind of work." That's the way it is in non-profits. I thought that it was a great experience working on the disaster action teams. It really taught me a lot, because disasters never follow a script, ever. You get situations where you have no idea what to do when the team is calling you from the field. One time, I got a call that a woman's house had just burned down. The woman had Alzheimer's, and her caretaker wasn't sure if she was in the country legally and was freaked out that the police were on their way. She was going to "take off." It was around two in the morning. At that point, I had to make a decision about what needed to be done. There was no time to be self conscious or worried about the fact that I didn't have the right leadership skills. I just had to jump into it. I just had to imagine that it was my own Mom in that situation and to think, "What do I want?" and

"How do we solve this?" There was no time to doubt. I just had to fix it.

Jennifer

I have volunteered on and off over the years. I haven't had time lately to roll up my sleeves and be hands-on, but my husband and I donate to organizations that we believe in. Before I had kids, I volunteered at a place called the "Peace Garden." It's in South Central Los Angeles, and it's a safe place for kids to hang out and have fun. I was involved in building the actual garden. It was very rewarding. When my kids get older, I probably will get involved again and get them involved as well.

How has volunteerism helped me? I think it flows back and forth. You can bring work leadership skills to volunteerism and the qualities of volunteerism to work, such as the quality of compassion. Overall, I just think it makes you a more well-rounded person.

Lane

Volunteering taught me to relate to people in a different way. I had been handed a lot of responsibility at a very young age, and volunteering gave me an outlet to have fun and be an equal within a team. It was also exciting to come together with other people for like-minded causes. For example, I spent a lot of time volunteering for film festivals. It was not only a great cause for the artistic community and for upcoming artists, but was also a good way to make contacts. Volunteering in general has always given me new and refreshing perspectives that I could bring back into the job.

Alma

My very first contact with the organization I've been working with for 30 years was as a volunteer helping to screen clients for the lawyer referral service. Similarly, several of our staff had volunteered with us before they were hired. Volunteering is a great way to get to know an organization and to put yourself in position for strong consideration if a job becomes available. You have an inside track, and you've been tested. They know you, and, if you're paying attention, you already understand the purpose and mission of the company.

In terms of leadership, we're always working with volunteers who help us with a variety of programs, such as planning new projects, screening and counseling clients, training mediators, or expanding our advocacy. While fostering a spirit of cooperation, we are trying to improve our services and have the greatest impact possible. Because we work with many volunteers in all of our programs, we really have intrinsic respect for them.

It's also important for people who have any sort of leadership position to be involved in their communities, to go beyond their job descriptions or the organizational mandate, and reach out to help others or contribute to community improvement. I have been on several boards and task forces throughout my career at C.L.A. That volunteer work informs my own work and helps me better understand what's going on in the community, while giving me a broad network of relationships. In creating new programs, like our arts and environmental initiative and our arts and community development program, we have had city and community support because people already know what we do and appreciate our efforts.

For example, I was appointed by the Mayor of San Francisco to the Citizens' Advisory Committee for Hunters Point Shipyard and served as a volunteer member for about 15 years. This group provides community oversight for the redevelopment of a decommissioned Navy base in the community I live in—Bayview Hunters Point. This is a typical community function for redevelopment projects. As a member of the Committee, I advocated preserving space for the arts at the base, which contains one of the largest concentrations of artists' studios on the West Coast. Eventually, C.L.A. organized and led a facilitated meeting involving artists and community members to develop programs of mutual interest. Some of the ideas which were generated are still in place after more than 10 years, such as providing a residency studio every year for a community artist who could not afford to rent a studio at the base. When we began our community development program placing disadvantaged high school students in summer internships in the arts, I turned to fellow members of the committee for advice, support and referrals. Recently, we started placing neighborhood kids in apprenticeships with artists who work in studios at the base.

I have also served on several art boards, like California Arts Advocates, the San Francisco Opera, and The Museum of the African Diaspora, as well as the San Francisco Human Rights Commission. When we have issues before local or state government agencies, or even the National Endowment for the Arts, we have a strong network of allies to call on for advice and support.

Melanie

The biggest transformation for me as a leader, and also as a human being, came through my volunteer work in the Soka Gakkai International world peace organization (SGI). This organization, based on the value-creating and humanistic philosophy of Buddhism, taught me how to overcome my negative tendencies and how to become a better, more contributive person.

Through SGI, I learned that leadership isn't about changing or manipulating others for your own personal needs or ego gratification. That never changes anything. The only way to change your environment or your circumstance, or even your destiny, is to change your inner condition first.

Over the past 27 years that I've been with the SGI organization, I've received incredible training on how to be a truly compassionate leader. If I didn't have that experience, I could never have had, let alone succeed in, the job I have today—never in a million years. I would not know how to conduct myself, how to help others, how to support others, how to build relationships, how to advance, or how to unite people as a team—all the things that are necessary for leadership and business. Honestly, I would not have had the courage to take on major responsibilities for which I had no formal education and no training. In that sense, it is because of my experiences in SGI that I have learned how to challenge myself and how to develop from within the courage and the confidence to learn on the job, to have the humility and to just keep on growing.

My feeling is that the human being comes first, over any job title or salary. I believe if you develop your humanity first, then it is very natural to become a leader in whatever capacity, in whatever your chosen field, and within your family. My practice of Buddhism has helped me transform and overcome the negativity and resistance I once held towards others. Today, I have really positive, loving family and social relationships. I can deeply appreciate others for who they are, not who I want them to be. Additionally, I can now offer leadership at times of great difficulty, such as emergency situations or with family crises that arise.

Volunteerism is not only an altruistic act, but it can also be quite beneficial for current and future leaders who want to adopt a more effective and compassionate approach to leadership. As the panel's answers demonstrate, volunteer work can help in three main ways by: 1) developing a person's leadership skills, 2) leading to better job and networking opportunities, and 3) enhancing a person's perspective.

*1. **Developing leadership skills:** Whether or not one takes a volunteer leadership position, volunteering, in general, is very helpful in developing leadership skills. For Elizabeth, her work with Red Cross Disaster Services taught her a lot about how to be a leader. For example, she was thrown into situations where she had to think on her feet and to act quickly in order to help others. Because of that experience, Elizabeth is now better able to deal with any crisis at the workplace in a compassionate manner.*

Melanie got a lot of her training by taking on leadership roles within her Buddhist community. Many faith-based organizations come from a place of compassion, and so taking on leadership positions in that capacity will naturally show a person how to use compassion in many effective ways. Because of her experience as a Buddhist leader, Melanie knows now how to help and support others as well as build relationships and unite people as a team. Melanie also feels that she learned how to challenge herself in a variety of ways so that she can now take on jobs for which she has had no formal training.

Taking a volunteer leadership position also leads to better diplomatic skills. Since volunteers are not getting paid, one has to exercise more charisma to persuade a team of equals and make decisions on their behalf.

Clearly, volunteering is quite invaluable in terms of acquiring skills for compassionate and highly effective leadership.

2. Job and networking opportunities: *Acquiring skills through volunteerism can naturally lead to other opportunities. For Alma, her volunteer work at the California Lawyers for the Arts put her in a great position when a job came available there. Many non-profits use volunteers, and it is a great way to put your "foot in the door." I would also add that putting volunteer work on a resume and the job skills you acquired during that experience helps as well. As Lane and Alma point out, volunteering is a great way to network. If it is in your field of interest, you may meet others who might just help you one day. For Lane, helping out at film festivals gave her opportunities to meet others in that industry. Alma, as an executive director of* *a non-profit organization, serves on city boards and other non-profits where mutual assistance comes into play for all involved. For example, by volunteering for the City of San Francisco, Alma was able to get city support for her organization's art programs.*

*3. **Enhancing perspective:** Volunteerism is also invaluable because it enables the person to see things from another, and sometimes more enlightened, perspective. For Lane, it gives her the opportunity to relate to others in a different way. As a leader, she does not get many opportunities to be an equal within a team, and the volunteer experience enhances her perspective. For Alma, volunteering informs the work that she does and gives her a broader perspective for other opportunities for the organization that she represents. Jennifer believes that the compassionate acts of volunteerism contribute to her becoming not only a better leader, but a more well-rounded person. In Melanie's experience, she was able to develop her humanity as well as overcome her negativity and resistance towards others. Because of that, she can better relate to others in a more humane and compassionate manner, not only in the workplace, but in other areas of her life.*

As in the student organizations mentioned earlier, leadership in a non-profit or volunteer organization is not based on financial reward. For this reason, leading volunteers can serve as another valuable lesson in inspiring a team beyond the profit motive. Certainly, financial reward can be a powerful incentive for motivating an employee or team member, but it is only one aspect of any job and usually the most mundane. To inspire an individual, a leader would do well to consider more than a team member's instinct for financial survival or enrichment. Other than money, what reasons might a person have for taking a particular job? Perhaps a person is interested or excited by the type of work done by a company, the same way they are excited by an interest or hobby. Maybe they enjoy working with people, learning something new, or contributing to a better world. These are the sorts of things that involve the whole person and appeal to each person's higher sense of oneself. Engage a person on these higher levels, and you will find a truly motivated, creative, and effective contributor to the team's goals. And these are exactly the types of motivational skills that one can learn in a student or volunteer organization.

MOTHERHOOD

How has being a mother helped you become a better leader?

Jennifer

I think you learn priorities and what is actually a crisis and what really isn't. You learn to put everything into better perspective. Now for me, stress is having a child who is really ill, as in, you have to take them to the hospital or they are throwing up on you on an airplane. That's real life stress. So when you get to the office, you realize, "Okay, with what I do, it's only television and it's all for entertainment. It's not something to get worked up or upset about." There are always stresses and there are deadlines, but there are always solutions. I feel that, at work, you can be in much more control than when you are at home with kids, where you never know what's around the corner. You are hit with a surprise every day. It really puts everything into perspective. I am much calmer at the office now and realize that a crisis at the office isn't really a crisis; it can be handled and there's always a solution. It's not the end of the world.

Lane

Being a mother is a lot harder than being a leader because it is so intensely personal. At work, you have protocol and systems in place that give you space and objectivity to be able to handle the crises that come up. It is, in many ways, routine. I thought that since I had been a leader, I could pretty much do anything, but I found out that being a mother is much more difficult. If you can handle being a Mom, you can handle anything that the workplace will throw at you. Many things that you learn while dealing with your children (patience, determination, rational thought) will make you a better leader.

Alma

Sometimes my experience as a parent does come in handy in getting people to understand the consequences of their behavior. With my children, I tried to lay down a foundation of cooperation and the consequences of non-cooperation. If people understand the consequences of their actions, they can then make the right choices. Providing the opportunity for voluntary cooperation and right choices, acknowledged with praise, help to build a harmonious team. It is certainly more productive and easy-going than a negative, punitive environment.

In the workplace, it may take time to help a person understand a situation completely. It must be done in a way that is not threatening, because when you threaten people, they shut down and communication stops. The important thing is for the team members to understand that I want to give them a chance to do the right thing, not just because I said so or because of some external threat, but because they know I care about them and want what is best for their future. At the end of the day, if their interests are aligned with the goals of the organization, the result is a positive, win-win situation for everyone.

Being a mother is probably the most altruistic role a woman can take. As the mothers on the panel will attest, it is also perhaps the most humbling. Like volunteering, motherhood not only enhances your leadership skills, but also gives you a more enlightened perspective.

Since being a mother is deeply personal, the women on the panel had no choice other than to deal with their children's issues. They couldn't just sit back, but had to take action. Because of the urgent needs of motherhood, they all found that they were capable of taking on leadership skills in a very personal way. For Lane, the job of being a mother seemed a lot harder than that of being a leader at work. In motherhood, there were no work rules or procedures for Lane to follow; she had to develop patience and learn how to be very rational at all times. Through motherhood, Jennifer learned how to think on her feet during a crisis. Now, at work, she can react to situations in a much calmer and compassionate manner when something is going awry. In Alma's case, she draws on her true-life motherhood experiences when trying to help employees understand the consequences of their actions. As she learned from raising her children, too, it helps to explain things in a kind and non-threatening manner, so the person will understand that you have his or her best interests at heart.

Motherhood also gives one an enlightened perspective when it comes to work. As Jennifer points out, you learn that a crisis at work is not really significant compared to, say, the problem of a sick child. As a mother, the unexpected is always coming at you. In fact, compared to the challenges of motherhood, the work place can be a place of safe refuge where things are more easily controlled.

Finally, if you can handle motherhood, then you definitely have the potential for being a good leader who is wise, compassionate, and effective. Motherhood is truly compassionate leadership in action!

CHAPTER 4

Learning from Mentors

Studies show that one of the best ways to learn about leadership is from mentors.[8] *Good mentors don't necessarily tell us what to do, but they show us behaviors that we can bring into the workplace as examples of what to do and how to treat people while coming from a place of compassion and real purpose.*

Tell me about the great bosses, mentors, or role-model leaders in your life. What made them great, and what lessons did you learn from them?

Jennifer

My former boss, Jeff Gaspin from NBC, was really a great example to me. He promoted me from Director to Vice President when I was working at NBC in the movie department. At the time, Jeff was in charge of movies and alternative programming, which covered reality shows. He had an open door and always knew when I was growing restless for more responsibility or change. At one point I wanted a change, and I went to him and said, "If you need any help covering a reality show, let me know. I'd be happy to get involved in that, too." He knew I was looking for new challenges, and there was an open slot in reality programming, so he said, "Why don't you just move into Reality full-time?" So I did. Jeff was a good role model because he really let me grow at my own pace and allowed me to be very honest with him. He also gave me a lot of freedom to put a show together. He would give me constructive notes on how I could improve the project, and I would take them and do what I could with them. I really trusted his instincts, so that was great. He was a great sounding board, too. To this day, I know Jeff is still there willing to give me advice.

My current boss, Nick Emmerson at Shed Media US, also gives me the space and responsibility to continue to develop as a leader. He has created an environment where it feels like he's more of a partner than a boss. He gives me a lot of freedom, which is great.

I would also count my old friend Jamila Hunter into this mix as someone who helped me as well. She and I worked at NBC together back in 2000-2003. We started off in television movies together and have always given each other the "reality check" that we need when we are in any kind of career crisis. We don't know how to *not* be honest with one another. She gave me a little paperweight once that said, "If you could do anything you want, what would it be?" I love that paperweight, and that quote is, and has been, in the back of my mind whenever I've had to make the "next move."

Melanie

In my work with the SGI, I have had a great mentor in the president of the organization, Daisaku Ikeda, who is a constant source of encouragement and a great example of how to cherish people.

As for bosses, I have had really dreadful bosses and really wonderful bosses. At this time, I am working with a woman who is a great boss. She is very positive, respectful, and a real team player. She gives me a lot of freedom and a lot of creative space. I report to her about my team of seven people, so she needs me and appreciates me as well. I have a great working relationship with her. I can tell her directly if something is going to work or not or if we should go this way or that way. She and I are very *simpatico* and not just about Girl Scouts; we both take a holistic view of empowering girls who will be future leaders. We also work to engage mothers, fathers, and other adults to be in role model positions so as to help transform the communities that they live in. My boss has more education and more experience than I do with fund development, so I appreciate her as a thought partner. I am very happy to learn from people, so it is particularly wonderful when I can learn from a great boss.

Lane

When I was moving up in restaurant management, I actually liked most of my managers and learned different things from different ones, but I had a very strong sense of myself as a manager. There wasn't anyone in particular who stood out.

When I made the transition to being a commercial producer, though, a man named Sam Walsh was a mentor to me. He taught me everything about the business. He was the nicest man too. He would say to me, "I'll get you coffee. Don't worry. Sit right there." Because of his kindness and generosity, I would do anything for him. I worked with him for a long time and when I went out on my own, he would pass off jobs to me if he was too busy. He understood the business, and he was good about explaining it, and he treated me like an equal, not like an underling. It's a very hard field to break into, so if it wasn't for him, I wouldn't have had my production career. He made it happen for me, and I will be eternally grateful.

Alma

When I graduated from Middlebury as a history major, it was in the back of my mind that I might go to law school, but I was not aware of all the various career opportunities in law at that time—or even how to apply. I don't think I would have gone to law school without some encouragement from people who saw my potential and mentored me. When I was working in Washington, D.C., I met Sally Ann Payton through my work as a journalist at the Washington Star. She was one of the first

African-Americans to graduate from Stanford Law School, and she was working in the Nixon administration when I met her. She encouraged me to apply to Stanford, and I got in. Throughout my law school years, Sally continued to check on me and encourage me. She helped me put things in perspective, encouraged me to "be a star," and always lightened things up with her sense of humor. We continued to stay in touch as she began her academic career teaching at the University of Michigan Law School.

Another important mentor was Thelton Henderson, who was a Dean at Stanford Law School when I was there and later became a federal judge. As my advisor in a juvenile law clinic, he helped me understand the context of the legal system and helped me see that I could make a difference in the lives of my young clients. He continues to be a positive influence in my life—someone I can count on for advice and encouragement. What I learned from each of them was that lawyers really can make a difference. There is a pervasive legal structure in our society, and to protect yourself, your family, and your community, I was advised, you need to master it. You can defend, and you can also have a point of view. You can be an advocate. You can make an impact. After my experience as a journalist, I wanted to be more knowledgeable, and I wanted to make a difference. I was encouraged to pursue law because, although I didn't know exactly what I would do with it, it would be a great pathway for finding out. With the support of these mentors, I also learned that I could reach inside and do more with my life than I had initially thought possible.

As far as mentoring me during my career, I can't say enough about Steve Camber, who was head of the arbitration and mediation committee when I was hired at Bay Area Lawyers for the Arts to start the mediation program (we became statewide and changed the organization's name to California Lawyers for the Arts in 1987). Steve supported my promotion to executive director in 1981 and became the president of the board the next year. We had such a close working relationship that still endures—even after he stepped down from the board presidency more than two years ago. I could call him about any personnel or financial problem, brainstorm ideas for new programs and get his feedback for any organizational issues. Being executive director in any organization can be a very stressful, lonely experience, and it's been great to know that I was not steering the ship alone.

Elizabeth

I had a great boss by the name of Dr. Nasser Golshan at NASA's Jet Propulsion Lab (JPL) when I worked there. He had invented the law of orbiting satellites, which is a really big deal in the area of communication systems, and he was so smart. He was probably the smartest person I have ever met in my life, and he was very humble. He would constantly pull me aside and give me advice because he knew I didn't want to be a career scientist and knew I wanted to go into business. One time he said to me, "Elizabeth, smart people hire people who are smarter than themselves, whereas mediocre managers hire people who are not as intelligent so that they can feel superior." He would give me such really wise tips on a regular basis on how to manage people. I don't remember how long he had worked at JPL, probably his whole life, but he had never fired anybody. I think the reason was that he was really good at hiring people. When cuts were made to different programs, he would find these employees a job in some other department because he knew they were good people and wanted to keep them. It was interesting how he had never mis-hired in his whole time there.

I have a lot of female mentors. They are amazing. The generations that came before me did so much to kick in the ceilings and the barriers in their workplaces and just pave the road so that my generation could come in and feel comfortable as women. I am constantly amazed by their strength, too. My mother is a surgeon, and she became a surgeon at a time when women weren't surgeons, so I grew up with the feeling that women can do anything. My new company Anti-AgingGames.com has set up a way to honor these trailblazing women and all women. By visiting our website and typing in

"ThanksLadies" in the VIP code area, customers get 20% off the monthly rate.

Although the panel learned a lot from each of their parents, they had valuable lessons taught to them by others. The mentors, bosses, and role models in their lives inspired the panel to be even better than they thought they could be. They set examples and role modeled the compassionate and effective leadership that the panel would adopt themselves. These mentors inspired and offered encouragement at pivotal points in the panel members' lives and careers.

When Lane was starting out in her producing career, she was referred to a man who would selflessly share his wisdom and knowledge of the profession. The kindness that he showed her motivated her to do whatever she could for him, again showing how kindness is a great motivator.

For Elizabeth, her boss at JPL went out of his way to help and guide her with wise tips on how to manage her staff. He was not required to share his wisdom, but he saw Elizabeth's potential and sought to empower her.

Jennifer shares how her former boss at NBC let her grow at her own pace and allowed her to be honest with him without judgment. His compassionate actions would make such a lasting impression on her that she would later emulate him in his leadership methods.

Melanie shares how she is excited to learn from her current boss and how that helps her. For Jennifer, her current boss allows her freedom and a significant amount of responsibility, so it feels more like a partnership. He empowers Jennifer and is not threatened by her. He lets her shine in her own right.

For Alma, not only was her former boss at C.L.A. an inspiration and mentor to her, but so were other exemplary individuals who mentored Alma as a young woman. They not only helped Alma believe in herself, but encouraged her that she could make a difference and truly help others by being a lawyer.

Mentors come to us in other areas of our lives as well. Melanie brings up a highly regarded Buddhist leader whose compassionate ways have encouraged her and have shown her how to cherish others. Of course, such a role model is not only influential in the spiritual aspect of life, but demonstrates the importance of using compassion in all areas of life, even at the workplace.

Friends, too, can be mentors. They usually are more honest with us and have our best interests in mind. For Jennifer, it is a good friend who gives her "reality checks" and reminds her of her dreams and goals.

For Elizabeth, it is the women who paved the way before her. She uses her mother as an example of being a surgeon at a time when female surgeons were a scarcity, understanding that the earlier generations of women had to face a lot more adversity in order to succeed. Their "never give up" spirit inspired her and showed her that anything is possible. Such role models are truly inspiring and make us want to be just like them.

Finally, I would like to make the point that more men than women were mentioned as mentors in this section. One reason is that many men do understand that compassionate leadership is the most effective way to lead. Another reason is that women still do not hold as many high leadership positions as men and in many instances have been discouraged to use compassion to lead. That is changing though. One of the younger women in this book, Elizabeth, points out that many women have been great role models to her. Therefore, generations to come will more than likely have an equal amount of female and male role models.

CHAPTER 5

The Fear Factor –
Being Fearless, Not Feared

A lot of people may still lead by fear, not because that is the only way they know, but because they, themselves, are in fear. Because of their insecurities, bad leaders will lash out at their own employees. One of the top requirements of a compassionate and highly effective leader is to be confident in one's own style of leadership and not to rely on using fear as a way to motivate others. I asked the panel the following questions about fear, and they all offered great insight and stories about how one should never lead or be led by fear.

"A leader should be fearless but not feared." What are your thoughts on this statement? How have you dealt with overcoming your own fears in terms of leadership?

Elizabeth

Leading with fear is such an outdated way to lead. Some people are motivated by fear, but there are so many studies that show that when fear is used, people become less creative, and they become less resourceful. They actually start getting tunnel vision because of the adrenaline. In a lot of ways, it's emotional abuse, and people aren't going to function at their best. When I was getting my MBA at USC (University of Southern California), a lot of the students had full time jobs at the same time at Fortune 500 companies. They would share stories about how their bosses would go "psycho" on them in shockingly inappropriate manners. These executives are people who have MBAs, and they let themselves rage on their staff in a way that you cannot even say the word "team morale" without laughing at the hypocrisy involved. To me, people want to be motivated by success. Everybody wants to be part of a winning team. You are not going to bring out the best in people by motivating them through fear. You might be able to motivate someone to work faster and harder at a very simple task, but if the task requires any kind of complexity or strategic thinking, that person will perform at a lower rate. Using fear to lead is an outdated method of the industrial age. There's really no place for it in the information age when you have your people and their ideas as the most valuable commodity. The machine is now easy to replace.

I've seen what fear does to people too. Luckily, I haven't let it rule me. I have had bad managers who would be very young and very smart, but not have that much experience and be really insecure. The fact that I am smart and worked below them made them nervous, because I was going to see the mistakes they made. As for me, I don't mind when the person below me sees mistakes I make. I actually like it because that means I'm not catching my own mistakes. In the corporate world, though, there is so much pressure for people to be perfect. So, if there is somebody below them who is smart, who can see that they are making mistakes, that threatens them. When that happens, they start lashing out and they start becoming enraged. I frequently found myself in meetings where the conflict wasn't even about the work, but about the person in charge who really just wanted to subordinate me.

At one of my former jobs, there was one guy who had taken some credit for work that I had done and had let the boss assume that he had done the work himself. I went to this guy and said, "You threw me under the bus, took my work and took credit for it, and then bad-mouthed me so that I wouldn't have the credibility to tell the manager that you had taken my work." At first he back-pedaled, but I just stood firm and told him that he was only fooling himself. It was interesting, because he broke down and said, "I don't know why this place is turning me into this. I did not used to be this way." With a lot of fear and anxiety in the air, it's hard to be kind. It was interesting to see how fast he cracked. He said to me, "I'm not as nice as you are." I said, "I have anger urges too, but I choose to set them aside at work." You have to leave that stuff at the door. Anything you do and say is a choice. If you are someone who is fearful and feels the need to steal somebody else's work or put someone else down in order to make yourself look good, how far will that get you? Instead, you should just excel and be noticed that way. Unfortunately, that's still not the way it is in a lot of corporations. I think they need to rethink the ways they conduct business, though, because startup companies like mine, where everyone is not spending half their day covering their butts and being afraid, are spending the whole day actually working.

In terms of overcoming my own fears, I used to have a massive fear of public speaking. I actually thought about dropping out of business school during the first month when I learned that we had to give a presentation in front of the class every week. Every time I spoke, I couldn't sleep at all the night before. I met with my communications class professor and told her that I wanted to conquer this fear. She gave me some tips; she basically told me to keep practicing at every opportunity. A funny thing happens when you face one of your irrational fears directly: not only does the fear disappear, a number of important doors open. By chipping away at my fear of public speaking, I was able to enter the USC Business Plan contest, which required repeatedly speaking in front of large groups and highly critical judges. Anti-AgingGames.com won the business plan contest, and we received seed money to start the business. We also received a lot of exposure and made a lot of important contacts. I now speak regularly at business schools and organizations and have gotten very high ratings. I have two favorite topics that I like to speak about: "How to Keep Your Brain Young: Strategies for People Over 40" and "How to Start a Socially Responsible Business." I love how you can literally change the lives of the people listening in the audience. It's fulfilling on a very deep level.

Jennifer

Leading with fear is less effective. Some people may need that push, but it's not comfortable for me to lead with fear because I don't like to be treated that way.

In dealing with fear at the job, I think some of that comes with experience. If you are comfortable with yourself and how you do things, then you won't have that problem. If you're not comfortable and are in constant fear at your job, then something is not right, and you should leave.

I think that some people aren't realistic about the television industry either. Some positions are meant to be short-term positions. There are few network presidents who last for very long periods of time. So, you have to be willing to go into a job thinking, "Okay, I may not be here forever, but I'm not going to think about that. I'm going to think about how I can do a great job while I'm here."

If you feel like your job might be in jeopardy, it's time for you to have a talk with your boss. For me, if something doesn't work out, it's fine. I know I'll be okay; I'll land another job. When I've negotiated my deals, I've always had the opinion that, "Yeah, I really want this job, but if the deal's not right for me, I'm walking away." I'm not going to be desperate about it. You end up getting what you want with that attitude. You also take that attitude and confidence into the job. Of course, I've had situations where I've really wanted something and it didn't happen. I thought, "Oh no! That would have been great." Looking back, I realize it wasn't actually the right situation. I came to the realization at some point—maybe it just came with age and experience—that there is always another job out there.

Lane

I have a personal abhorrence of people who lead by fear. I find it unnecessary, for one, and simply vile, for another. I cannot abide by people who cannot manage to lead with respect, dignity, and humanity.

Back in my restaurant days, there was a corporate person who would interview people who wanted to become managers. This man believed in stress interviews where he would try to physiologically and psychologically trip you up. He would do things like position you so the sun would be in your eyes, so you would then have a hard time seeing and need to ask him to move. He would purposefully do things to throw you off your game to see if you were management material. Those types of tactics don't work for me. I believe the stresses of the job are different from the weird fake stresses used in such a test. Not to mention, they're insulting. I am a more humane type of leader. My first interview was with that particular corporate person, and I failed. As a result, I didn't advance in management that first time. They eventually got rid of him, and when I went back to interview the second time I did just fine.

Once I became a leader, I realized I had no fears about it. I was taught very well about how to lead in the restaurant business, so when the time came for me to lead my own team, it seemed like a natural progression. I was quite pragmatic about the job to be done and I looked forward to it.

Melanie

In certain jobs I've worked, it was a war-zone mentality: fight or flight. Most of my co-workers were in survival mode. I feel fortunate to have a different sensibility about life. In those kinds of work situations, how I acted and interacted with people was usually different. Number one, I wouldn't treat other people badly, and I wouldn't let people treat me badly. I would speak up. I don't care if you're the owner or the president, you can't say certain things to me. I draw a line. For example, when I worked in the film industry, I was working with men who were older and thought nothing of making sexist comments to women about their clothing, bodies, etc. I would not let those comments stand. Because I stand up for *myself,* it's very clear that I'm going to stand up for *others.* I don't allow anyone to mistreat anyone around me. I don't want to hear it. I've never felt that I ever had to sacrifice my integrity or somebody else's integrity to achieve something. I'm more into personal achievement than I am into reward. What personally motivates me is not necessarily what motivates someone else to move up a ladder.

My Buddhist practice over the years has helped me maintain that strong sense of identity and integrity amid the chaos of some pretty harsh work environments. I would say, though, that I've always had a sense of myself that started at a young age in my quest for independence. For example, after graduating college at the age of 20, I worked my way around the world for two years. I worked at odd jobs—anything I could find that would pay me and keep me traveling. I worked cleaning hotel rooms. I worked on a kibbutz in Israel. I worked with a circus in Ecuador. I taught English in Belgium. So, I never based my identity on my job or job status and was never dependent on a boss's opinion of me.

Alma

I once left a job because I was experiencing "supervision by intimidation." I don't think you get the best work from people if they feel that they're being threatened or unfairly criticized.

They shut down and you're going to get the least out of them. As a leader, it's better to try to understand people from a humanistic point of view and figure out what motivates them, and it's usually not fear.

As for overcoming my fears…well, I tell myself, and I have had to do this a few times, "Okay, you did not go to the school where they teach you to roll over and lie down. You have to get up and take a stand." So, I have a little conversation with myself because I am not a very aggressive person. I remind myself about the kind of training and education I've received, which is to be present and prepared at any moment to step up and take a position when it counts. And so, I have often gone against the odds, even when I was afraid of failing. Back in the 90's I worked hard, calling on colleagues around the country to reverse an NEA Chairman's decision not to fund our organization because he didn't think the NEA should fund legal services for artists. I've also worked with others and put our organizational resources on the line to try to restore state funding for the California Arts Council—so far, unsuccessfully. And I've gone way past my comfort zone in helping members of my family when they were confronting abusive situations. For example, when an elderly aunt's lawyer was stealing her life's savings, I employed all of the legal tools I could in order to make sure he was investigated, prosecuted and eventually convicted. Sometimes, you overcome your own fears when you need to support others and when you feel the cause demands it.

I've had many opportunities to play a meaningful role as an advocate. In addition, I've had the benefit of a great partnership with my husband, Toye Moses, who works for the City of San Francisco and serves as a community leader in many capacities. He founded the San Francisco African American Democratic Club and has served on several city commissions, including the Immigrant Rights Commission and the Mental Health Commission. We often share our political insights and come up with strategies for confronting challenging situations. He also encouraged me to start our youth internship program, which has placed more than 500 young people from low-income families in internships and apprenticeships in the arts. This project led to our much larger "CultureCore" program, which no longer exists, but served more than 5,000 youth with arts enrichment activities. C.L.A. was, in fact, the first arts organization to receive funding from the San Francisco Mayor's Department of Children, Youth and Families, which opened the door for all kinds of arts agencies to receive funding from that agency. Toye is always bringing me opportunities to get more involved in community issues, and in 2003 we were both installed as Chiefs in his village, Imasayi, in Ogun State, Nigeria.

As the panel concurs, leading by fear is the far less effective way to lead. Kind leaders know that and do not choose that form of leadership. They know that it is less effective, because they have experienced intimidation from their superiors in the past, and it did not work for them. Elizabeth shares how she witnessed people stealing credit and verbally abusing each other because of the pressures of their jobs. Those pressures made people fearful. Her conclusion was that people would accomplish more if they did not spend half their day just trying to cover their behinds. Lane had the experience of being interviewed with the intimidation of a physiological test to trip her up. The experience stayed with her, and as a result she feels that type of leadership is vile and unnecessary.

Melanie witnessed at earlier jobs the war-zone mentality of fight-or-flight. She noticed that her fellow employees were in a survival mode and that, luckily, she had a different sensibility. Alma left a job because she was experiencing intimidation. Alma makes the point that no one will do their best job if they are being threatened or criticized and that people shut down in those circumstances. It's not nice, and it's not effective. Jennifer experienced, too, that leading by fear was not the right method for her since she didn't like being treated that way herself.

These experiences may be part of it, but it is a conscious choice for these women to avoid leading by fear or intimidation. As stated in the introduction of this book, and by Elizabeth who has done research in this field, there are neurological studies that demonstrate people become less creative and less resourceful when experiencing fear. In many cases, using fear to lead amounts to emotional abuse. So, it goes without saying, leading with fear is not nice and it's not effective.

The best way to lead is not only without fear but, in fact, to be fearless. After all, in most cases, those who lead by fear are living in fear themselves. They are insecure and threatened by others who are smarter and more talented than they are. Their fear makes them lash out at others. Of course, no one can be completely free of fear, but it should be an aspiration of any good leader. If you let go of fear at the job, you will feel at ease and most likely be in a good mood most of the time. It will be easier to be kind and bring out the best in people. If you are fearless in terms of your job as a leader, you will not be threatened by people who might be smarter or more talented than you. In fact, a fearless leader will make an effort to get smarter and more talented people on his or her team. Now, that's nice. Truly kind leaders are fearless. In turn, fearless leaders inspire others by being great role models of compassionate and highly effective leadership themselves.

It is interesting that all of these women have experienced intimidation from fearful and fear-inspiring bosses in the past. For a practice that is so universally reviled, it appears to be very common. What this reflects is how common fear is in the human condition. No matter how much we would all like to avoid behaving out of fear, it is still a hard thing to accomplish. That is why practicing good leadership techniques, having mentors, and learning more about all the subjects covered in this book are so important.

In this chapter, too, the panel has shared how they overcame their fears. Elizabeth uses the example of public speaking and that the way to conquer a fear is to face it head on. In her case, she took advantage of every opportunity to speak publicly, and the result was that many new opportunities became available to her. Jennifer felt she came to the realization at one point, through age and experience, that there is always another job out there and was able to let go of a lot of fear. She offers the advice that one should never be desperate about a job while interviewing. If you are clear and confident about what you want, everything will work out. Lane relied on her training and experience to give her the confidence she needed to lead fearlessly. Of course, she was a leader in her family, so she feels leading came naturally and had no fears about it.

In Melanie's case, she used her Buddhist faith to keep her integrity and identity in tact. She doesn't live in fear because she doesn't rely on her bosses' opinions of her. One may not be a

Buddhist, like Melanie, but by having faith in oneself and keeping true to one's convictions, a person is less likely to dwell in a place of fear.

Alma uses self-talk to remind herself that she didn't go to the school that taught her to just roll over, but to take a stand when necessary. As a result, Alma has taken advantage of many opportunities to take a stand not only for herself but in conjunction with others on behalf of those in need in her family, community, and at large. Alma's amazing accomplishments are the proof of such fearless leadership!

These women's stories are inspirational because they admit to being fearful and show us through their own humility how to be strong and overcome our own fears. They are just like us and, with the compassion of a mentor, they show us that we too can empower ourselves to be strong and compassionate leaders.

CHAPTER 6

Qualities of Compassionate and Highly Effective Leadership

The final chapter of this section deals with what each woman on the panel views as great leadership qualities. Since these women have been selected for their kind and inspirational leadership, the qualities they list reflect that.

What do you think are the qualities of a great leader?

Lane

First of all, a leader has to be able to inspire trust. No one is going to want to follow you unless you are honest, forthright and people believe what you have to say. You must be credible. Secondly, a leader must be responsible. If you are in charge, then anything and everything that happens is your responsibility, and you must be willing to accept that. It must resonate with you, fulfill you, and keep you motivated. As a leader, I thrive on the responsibility and the potential that I feel my position offers for me to "do good" (as opposed to doing something well). Thirdly, a good leader is analytical. It is important to be able to break down whatever situation you are in to its most basic components. You must be able to see both the big picture and the small details that will make a difference to each outcome. In addition, you must plan your strategy and prioritize your actions to achieve your success. Fourthly, a good leader is calm and focused on the future. On the path toward your goals, you will have many obstacles! To be able to focus on the future and keep calm when dealing with setbacks are key. Also, remain thoughtful in the face of opposition. It will help you in determining what to learn from your obstacles and what to discard. Keeping calm will encourage others to do the same and will maintain your stance as a leader so you do not "fall apart." Lastly, it is so important to be enthusiastic and have fun with what you are doing. It simply cannot be hard work all the time. Reward yourself! Reward others! Take time to "smell the roses." All projects and processes are improved by a light-hearted approach and a sense of humor.

Jennifer

I would say patience, honesty, humanity, a good sense of fairness, a cool head, and loyalty are attributes of a good leader. It's great if a leader can have all these traits and it helps to be or try to be all these things. I don't always display all of these qualities, but I do aspire to them. As a leader, you must also be protective of your team. In the entertainment industry, there's so much change and there's so much uncertainty. For this reason, I feel like one of the most important things a good leader has to do is stand by his or her team and protect them and support them when someone on the team has messed up. No one is perfect; we all screw up. I have seen leaders behave both ways. One kind of leader is one who supports the team no matter what. Then there's the other kind of leader, who distances him or herself when someone on the team screws up, but has no problem taking credit if someone on the team does something really well. It is really important for a leader to be a good example. People look at behavior inside and outside the office for cues as to how they are supposed to behave and what's acceptable behavior. If you don't set a good example, you are grooming people to be poor leaders themselves.

Elizabeth

I think that a great leader needs to be serving others as opposed to serving him or herself. Most of the people that I have seen who are really great leaders are the ones who are just trying to help the company or non-profit or whatever they are leading, whereas the ones who are mediocre are thinking about themselves. Also, having integrity—being open and honest about the fact that you make mistakes—is a great quality to have. I have seen a lot of mediocre leaders pretend that they are perfect, but nobody is perfect. I have more respect for a person who makes mistakes and then admits it and fixes it, than for someone who pretends that he or she is perfect. So, I would say the need to help and integrity are up there on my list.

Melanie

I think there are certainly many qualities to being a great leader. I would say that honesty, integrity, and appreciation and respect for others are very important. Also, having the courage of your convictions in making decisions is critical. Ultimately, great leaders are not looking for their own empowerment, but rather to empower others, in the most humanistic sense, to reveal their own unique and individual greatness. When a person can lead in that way, the environment will be transformed, whether in the workplace, the neighborhood, or within the family. This transformation is truly the test of a really great leader.

Alma

A good leader is a person who listens and understands what the range of possibilities are—a person who can work from experience, and who has an idea of how to effect positive change in order to realize a vision.

Several years after I started working with California Lawyers for the Arts, our volunteers and staff did mediation training and helped other organizations start similar programs around the country. It is very exciting to be able to help somebody in another state or an artist in California who has a problem in New York. We were able to demonstrate, "Okay, the mediation program worked for artists here, so, let's see if we can solve problems across state lines." And so, having helped to develop that program, we have a certain sense of confidence that something good can happen beyond solving a problem for an individual or an organization. That is an example of leadership through having set up systems and processes where people who have needs can benefit. For another example, our organization tries to fill the gap for artists through educational programs to make sure they can first of all understand what their legal responsibilities are and then get the records and paperwork they need. We do not always manage to meet everybody's expectations, but I think we do a good job. Sometimes leadership is not just doing something yourself, but also setting up systems so that many people can be assisted.

The list of leadership qualities that the panel shares is not only about individual characteristics, but qualities that are important when working with others. As you read the rest of the book, you will see how these women implement these qualities in their daily leadership roles. I offer the following list to you as a condensed summary of the important leadership qualities mentioned by the panel:

Personal Qualities:

Honest, courageous, wise, compassionate, responsible, analytical, calm, foresighted, enthusiastic, a good role model, patient, fair, loyal, humane, has integrity, open, humble, a good listener, a decision-maker

Interactive Qualities:

Inspires trust, is loyal to team, protects the team, serves others, has a need to help others, has respect for others, empowers others, transforms the environment, seeks out smarter people, sets up systems so others can be helped, knows how to affect positive change, rewards others

While no one can be perfect all the time, this list might serve as a checklist and reminder of the kinds of qualities and goals to which we all should aspire in becoming highly effective and compassionate leaders.

PART II

LEADING A TEAM

CHAPTER 7

Choosing Members of Your Team

Hiring the right people and putting together a winning team is probably the first step of being a leader in business. More importantly, having great people on your team makes you look great as a leader. Here's how the panel does it…

How do you go about choosing a team?

Jennifer

Part of my job is hiring the team that is going out in the field executing the show. The first part of the hiring process is the first impression. When someone walks in the door and shakes my hand and says, "Hello," I don't decide immediately if it's the right person, but I can decide immediately if it's *not* the right person. My gut tells me a little bit. Basic interview skills are important, such as: they've really thought about what they're wearing; they're excited to be there; and they've actually done some research on the company. It's usually a long conversation. If it feels like a one-sided interview, then I know that connection isn't quite there. If it flows easily and I can see myself wanting to spend time with this person, that's important, because sometimes in this business we end up spending more time at the office than at home. Then I check people out.

I'll call a couple of people with whom they've worked. I may not use the references they give, either. If I see on the resume that they've worked at a certain place, and I know someone there really well, I'll call that person. I think it depends on how smart the person is and if he or she is qualified without saying it. Another thing to consider is whether or not the person will mesh with the group and the philosophy of the company. What I love about this company [Shed Media US] is that it's not a company driven by ego. In past jobs, I've had to deal with a lot of egos. So, with job candidates, it's hopefully a "no egos" zone.

Melanie

I look for someone who is being honest with me, first, and foremost. For example, I hired a grant writer; I told her what the salary was and she started laughing. I said, "I know, it's a joke." She said, "Well, then you can't afford me. With that salary, I can only work part time." I said, "Fine with me. I don't care if you are here, or you are at your home desk. I could care less as long as you are able to do the work, and in the manner in which we need it done. If you want to come in on a part-time basis and work once or twice a week, that's fine." After all, it's non-profit. So, I look for someone who is honest right away, even people who tell me, "I have never done that, but I feel like I could learn it." I look for integrity as much as possible, and, of course, skill and experience. I am not going to interview just anybody. I try to gauge integrity, personality, experience, as well as flexibility. I let people know that there are times when we work as a team and cover for each other. We may have extended hours when we have a big project, and I have to ask, "Is this going to be a problem for you?" I try to give them as much information upfront as possible. Recently, I hired somebody for a position that had been open for a while. It was down to two people, and I brought them both back for second interviews. One person was very bright, very detail oriented, and very assertive, and she was looking for training and opportunity. I really liked her, and I really felt that I could work well with her, but the bottom line was that she had to be able to fund-raise. I really drilled down on this point and asked, "Are you comfortable with making cold calls and going after people, building relationships from scratch and being able to sponsor events?" I could see she started to hesitate. Later, she wrote me a "thank you" note and said that she decided to stay with the place where she already was. You have to make your best, educated judgment and really speak to the specifics of what the job responsibility entails. I have made hiring mistakes in the past. At this point in my career though, I would rather keep a position open for months than hire someone who is inappropriate for the job. If you hire the wrong person, you end up doing twice as much work and then having to undo the problems they created.

Lane

In the restaurant business, when hiring a server, I really looked for an individual who was naturally positive, a "people-person," in order to depend on him or her to respond to people the right way. Otherwise, the job was so simple that you could teach anybody to do it if they had even a modicum of smarts. During the interview process, I would ask people what their good experiences were and what their bad experiences were, and people would tell me stories. From the stories, I could determine whether or not they had a positive view of the world.

When I was working as a producer, I was hiring designers, composers, and editors. I was luckier in that regard, because there is a freelance pool there and you can test people out before you hire them. You want to know what kind of people they are but you are also interested in what their skills are, where they want to go, and what their expectations are. You can ask them a lot of questions regarding their creative talents and experiences. You can see portfolios of their work and have a chance to work with them on a project or two before you make a commitment to them.

As for building a team, I like to think about the whole as well as the individual parts. I don't want to hire the same kinds of people with the same weaknesses. Everybody has things that they do well and things that they do less well.

You try to average that out and balance it up. Maybe somebody is much more precise but a little bit slower in how he or she approaches things. Somebody else is really fast but makes more mistakes. You are never going to get "perfect-perfect." Everybody has fabulous things about themselves; you want to try to bring out the best in everybody in the way that you assign projects to them and bring balance to your team.

In the design world, specifically, there is the issue of talent and who is a good fit for a job. You really need to pay attention to the person that you hire for a particular project and make certain they are the exact fit for the project before you commit to the project itself. For example, if a client really needs to be handled gently, then you want a designer that you know has the patience to deal with that. If a project requires a specific software skill set, it's important to verify a designer's experience level with that software. Is he Einstein or Elmer Fudd—or somewhere in between? There are so many different qualities to consider prior to a hire.

Alma

At California Lawyers for the Arts, we try to find people who understand our mission and really have a passion for helping people, especially artists. Many times they are themselves artists and have some sort of empathy for emerging artists and entertainers—our primary constituency. They may have gone to law school and may be interested in mediation or education work. There is a huge range of talents and interests among the people who have come to work in our organization, and it has really been interesting to have people with different backgrounds and even different artistic backgrounds working alongside each other to try to figure out how to get our message out and how to educate our constituents. Trying to find the best person for the particular function is one thing, but we also hope that they embrace our mission and have a sense of humor. That's important because everything cannot be life-and-death serious or we wouldn't be able to help anybody. Since we have to be able to have some distance from what's going on, a sense of neutrality and humor often help.

Elizabeth

I look for people who have really good priorities. For example, the neuropsychologist I hired for my company [Anti-AgingGames.com] had flown out here with his family on vacation. While I was interviewing him, his daughter came up and said, "Daddy, you promised that you would put this [Crackerjack] tattoo on me." She held out the tattoo patch, and he stopped in the middle of the interview and said, "I will be right back. I am sorry." He left, put the tattoo on his daughter, and came back. Before that, I was thinking I was going to hire him because he was really smart, very interested and extremely passionate about the subject of using games and information to potentially slow down aging. When he took care of his daughter, he did it with kindness and caring—he didn't rush putting on the tattoo at all, he just took care of it. He came back and said, "Sorry, I had to do that. Where were we?" I just knew we were going to hire him on the spot, because here was a guy who puts his family first. If he puts his family first, there is a really good chance that he is also going to put his customers first. If he puts that same level of care into whatever he touches, it's going to be fantastic. I did hire him, and, to this day, every time we create a game he is very careful to say, "How does this affect this age group versus this age group?" He acts like the customers are his own kids or his own family. That's how much he cares, fundamentally. So, I look for people who are honest, passionate and respectful. Everything else can be *trained*.

What does hiring a staff have to do with kind and effective leadership? As the old Hollywood adage goes, "Ninety percent of a director's job is casting." One of the most effective ways to lead is to create a situation where a talented and well-matched group of people is enabled to cooperate in a productive and creative way. This type of pre-planning avoids potentially unproductive conflicts and failures down the road and makes a leader's job much easier. If you choose the wrong people, you are not being nice to anyone, let alone yourself.

The women on the panel give good guidance on what to look for when choosing a team. All agree it starts with the interview process and first impressions count. Some people look good on paper, but meeting them can be another story. Even though previous job experience is important, the panel feels that certain personality qualities are even more important. Why? Because you can train people for a job, but you can't teach people such qualities as honesty, integrity, compassion, intelligence, loyalty, flexibility, and being respectful. Nor can you teach them to be team players or to understand and mesh with the mission and philosophy of the company. These are qualities you may find in kind and effective leaders (as mentioned in the previous chapter), but they are also the qualities of kind and effective employees. For example, you want members of your team to be honest, so you know you can trust them. Also mentioned was the fact that you spend most of your day with your staff, so you should hire people you would not mind spending time with.

How do you know a candidate has such wonderful qualities when you meet them for the first time? The panel agrees it comes down to having a gut instinct about the person. Elizabeth's story of how a man she was about to hire stopped the interview for a few minutes to help his daughter is a great illustration of this point. Elizabeth could see that if this man could put his family first, then he would put the customer first as well. If the man scolded his daughter for interrupting him, another kind of leader may have thought that man was just doing what a father should do. Elizabeth saw it differently, though; she saw a man with good priorities. While interviewing, most people do no get the advantage that Elizabeth had to see the person in action. It may be hard to figure out if a person will be the right one for the job from the get-go. As Jennifer says, it usually requires a long conversation and then going back and checking all possible references. Melanie makes the point that sometimes she will keep a position open for a while until the right person comes along. Some on the panel had the advantage of hiring freelance help first, which, if possible, is a good option. That way, both of you, the leader and the new employee, can see whether the job is the right fit.

In regards to team building, you have specific positions that you must fill. You also have to assess the skills needed on the team and then look for individuals who possess those specific skills, but who also have the right general skills. Of course, Lane makes the point, too, that the people you hire should complement each other and not share the same weaknesses.

Therefore, as the panel concurs, putting together a team is an important task for any leader. The most effective and compassionate approach in selecting a team is to find the best possible people for each position who will complement each others' strengths. If you do that and provide the right environment, you will more than likely succeed as a leader and be quite productive.

CHAPTER 8

Leading an Existing Team

Leaders are put to the test immediately when they join a team or staff that is already in place. It is a difficult challenge, especially when the previous leader did things quite differently. How a new leader handles such a delicate situation is important. The panelists share their methods.

Sometimes you are put in charge of people whom you didn't choose. How have you handled this?

Lane

I have led many teams that did not know me, and I have had to earn their trust. It just takes some time, and you have to get to know them a little bit. You have to make them appreciate your good qualities, admire you, and respect you, because you want them to stand up for you and be a productive part of your team. You want them to bring things to you and communicate with you in order to build a strong team. You have to prove to them that you're listening to them and that you're paying attention and that you will do good by them. You also have to be firm, but fair, with people. Sometimes, after the process of getting to know each other and having analyzed the needs of the situation, you have to rearrange people, bring new people in, and let some people go. It just depends. I have never been one of those people who, when I walk in, needs to get rid of everyone and bring in my own team. Although being able to hand pick a team is really a treat, I think I can work with just about anybody.

Alma

I was initially hired to start and direct the mediation program at California Lawyers for the Arts, and I was so excited about it. I actually went to the office a day ahead of schedule, and everybody was working on a mailing. I just pulled up a chair and said, "Oh, I love this. May I help out?" and became a member of the team. When you do that, people understand that you are willing to do anything alongside them. Eventually, when I was appointed executive director and became their leader, I had already earned their respect through mutual support and teamwork. Everybody was respectful, because we were all working towards the same goals and supporting each other. That's the kind of working relationship I enjoy. You have to be part of that give-and-take rather than telling people what to do or exactly how they should do every aspect of their job. I hope that I have been successful in motivating people at another level, and I hope I lead by example on that. It's not about becoming a workaholic, but really enjoying the work and enjoying sharing the challenges and successes with other people.

Melanie

Actually, with the job I'm at now, three out of the seven team members came with the position, so to speak. It was a hard transition because, of those three, one of them in particular was basically doing my job in another Girl Scout council. (Girl Scouts of Greater Los Angeles is the result of merging six independent Girl Scout councils.) In other words, we had the same level position and worked together on the new organization structure for a year and a half in advance of the actual merger.

This woman and I had been team partners, at the same level, and then I became her boss. That was very challenging for me as well as for her. It took me some time to feel comfortable with being her boss, honestly, because we had been friends. Before the merger, it was just very fun and social. I had to grow into being her boss, and she had to grow into being part of my team. I have tried to encourage her, and I have really tried to appreciate her. Many things have changed, and part of the job that she was expecting to do has been taken away from her. Someone else was hired to do that piece because it was too much work for one person. She felt slighted by the job change and that we hadn't given her an opportunity. I really try to embrace her, listen to her, and make her feel appreciated. I think appreciating people is a part of leadership and, very naturally, if you are looking for support as a leader, you have to support others. I try to support each person in his or her own unique manner and, at the same time, make it clear that I need his or her support to be able to advance in a certain direction or to achieve certain goals.

Jennifer

I think you have to embrace a team when you come into a new situation or place. I go in with an open mind and try my best to trust them from the start. Until something happens to disappoint, you should give people a chance.

When my boss, Jeff Gaspin, came to NBC as the new head of the movie and alternative (reality) department, I was already part of the team. He could have "cleaned house" and brought in his own team, but he didn't. He trusted that we knew what we were doing and gave us all a shot, and he never made us feel like we were auditioning for him. I think that's a real talent and really positive role model behavior because not everyone behaves that way. As a result, we all stuck around for a really long time.

Elizabeth

I was hired at JPL-NASA to do science research working on the intersection between science and graphics, which is satellite imaging. Within a month, though, I had found a data set that was numerical and not image-based, and I told my boss that this data set was much better. I told him we should use that data set for various reasons, such as better coverage, and better resolution for what he wanted to do. He told me that I had just put myself out of a job, because in the department there were nothing but Caltech PhD's who were much better with numerical analysis than I could ever be, and I was hired to do satellite imaging. I told him I knew that, but nonetheless this numerical data was much better in terms of data set. As a result, he promoted me to lead the new project, which was a crazy five-year leap for me. I had a team who helped me with the study. It was a little strange at first; I walked into the room and everybody else on the team were men who were probably 30 to 50 years older than I was—I was in my mid-twenties at that time. These PhDs were surprised that someone who was not only younger, but with merely a bachelor's degree was hired to manage the task!

They were fairly friendly, although one of the men on my team was a bit grumpy about the whole thing. Although I showed him that I was really capable and continually acted kind to him, he did harass me on a regular basis. Whenever I would make presentations, he would pick the smallest, most insignificant item, and he would say something like, "What's that spot of data from July 7 to July 10, 1997?" and so on. Because he would grill me, and I had such a fear of public speaking and was the only bachelor's degree in the room *and* the only woman, I would have heart palpitations as I spoke. I got into the habit of preparing extra information, so whenever he would ask a question like, "What about this data point back in 1996?" I was prepared. I would have an answer like, "Well, that's a rain storm that happened, and the telescope was closed during that period." Once he knew I had the information, he stopped asking. I think he stopped because he was actually making me look good by grilling me in front of everybody, since I knew the answers. He also learned that my work was as good as my boss thought it was, and he finally backed off for good. I think one of the reasons I got good recommendations and good evaluations was because he was grilling me "hardcore" and people saw that I was handling it calmly and with kindness. I was taking his questions and answering them in a capable way and if I didn't know the answer, I would say, "I don't know, but I will get back to you on that," and I would. It's funny how the guy who was giving me such a hard time actually ended up helping me in the end, inadvertently. There's not much you can do when people challenge you like that. You might as well just choose to figure out what your values are and come from a place of your own values, especially when other people are behaving badly.

I found it quite wonderful that all of the women came into these situations from a place of compassion and tried to embrace the existing team. As Lane and Jennifer mention, some leaders come in and "clean house," but none of these women did that. Many leaders are hired to come in and fix things. Of course, an easy way out would be to start over with a new staff, but the panelists tried to work with the people they already had. Undoubtedly, this choice provided a compassionate example to the team, boosting morale and encouraging productive cooperation in the future.

The panelists did this in a variety of ways. Jennifer goes in with an open mind and tries to really embrace her new team. If changes need to be made, Lane makes the point that moving people around into different spots may just do the trick, and you may discover that people have qualities and talents that were previously untapped. Also, empowering people is extremely important. You do this by earning their trust and respect through listening and caring about the jobs that they do. Alma's story about how she went to work a day before the job started and joined the staff in stuffing envelopes is a wonderful story of how a good leader bonds with her new team. By doing that, Alma felt that she established camaraderie and became a part of the team, while setting a good example.

Melanie and Elizabeth share stories about challenges with specific individuals, showing that transitions are not easy but can be made to work. Melanie had a delicate situation where her equal became her subordinate. Melanie did not play a power trip on this individual; instead, she came from a place of compassion and listened and encouraged her. Melanie emphasized the point of truly appreciating and supporting not only this one individual but all of the members of her staff. By doing that, Melanie created an atmosphere of mutual appreciation and support.

Elizabeth's story of leading a study at JPL-NASA was truly challenging since she was heading a team of older men with higher degrees. She also was in no position to fire anyone, so she had to make the best of the situation. Even though the majority of the men did support Elizabeth, it turned out to be of great benefit to her that one of the men on the team did challenge her. His constant questioning of her abilities made her more prepared so that eventually she got great reviews and recommendations. Now, that is a good story showing that sometimes our greatest nemesis can turn out to be our greatest ally. A weaker and less compassionate leader may not have thought so.

Jennifer's experience as an employee gaining a new boss, Jeff Gaspin, when she worked in the movie department at NBC, shows how important it is to role model the best behavior possible in those situations. As other women in the panel have demonstrated by their own experiences, Jeff demonstrated for Jennifer how to behave when leading a new staff. Jennifer felt that Jeff gave everyone a chance and trusted that they all knew what they were doing. Such an experience was great leadership training for Jennifer.

Finally, the women make the point that by getting an existing team on your side, your staff will open up, feel inspired, share ideas with you, and do their best job possible. With the benefit of such a committed and motivated staff, a new leader will then be able to put her imprint on things and lead in her own way. In some of these cases people were let go, but it was all for the benefit of the entire team. Sometimes, that's actually the nicest choice for everyone involved.

In each case, the women achieved the best results by putting their egos aside and doing what was best for the team, leading in the most compassionate and effective way possible.

CHAPTER 9

Delegation and Control – Too Much vs. Too Little

I put the subjects of delegation and control in the same chapter because each relates to the other. As a leader, you must delegate or distribute the tasks of every job to the proper individuals on your team. As a leader, though, you are the one who is in control and therefore ultimately responsible for those jobs you have delegated. The panel shares their thoughts on delegation and control.

DELEGATION

As a leader, you want the individuals in your team to grow, so you must delegate. Please share how you delegate. How do you know you delegated too much versus too little?

Jennifer

You have to delegate and trust people to do their own jobs. I like to let go, but I also like to keep an eye on things and check-in to make sure things are headed where they need to head. Because I'm a bit of a control freak by nature, it's hard for me to delegate sometimes, but I know it's something I have to do.

Lane

When I owned the restaurant chain, I had to do a lot of delegating because we were open from 6 a.m. until 11 p.m. There was no way I could be there all the time, and so I had to train people to count money, to make bank deposits, etc. I also had to have other people who knew how to train people to be cooks and train people to be servers, and I had to have people who could run things during my absence. I had to delegate a lot of responsibility to other people, and it isn't something that you can do just like that. It's not like one day you are an employee, and the next day you are counting money and taking it to the bank. You really have to ease people into it and make sure that they are ready and that they're responding properly. It's important to keep people challenged, but not overwhelmed; they need to feel ready to take on the next level of whatever it is. You are walking that fine line the whole time that you're trying to bring people along. How quickly you move them along is also dependent on the task, whether it's just going from supervisor to manager, or, in the design business going from a junior designer to designer or from designer to lead designer. You have to watch carefully to make sure that the person is ready to take on the new task and that he or she is responding to situations correctly.

Melanie

I think it is just trial and error. You need to see someone's capacity and sometimes that is not clear. Sometimes, you are pleasantly surprised and think, "Wow, they are much more capable than I had given them credit for." Everyone has their own specific responsibilities. There are specific goals they must meet and expectations that they must achieve. If they don't do something well or correctly, I work with them. At the same time, if someone on my team wants to try new things or wants to take more creative opportunities, I always give that team member the opportunity. They will enjoy their job if they are excited and challenged.

Alma

I tend to work on the volunteer theory. I'll ask, "Will somebody help me do such and such?" or "Who is interested in working on this new thing?" and people usually come forward to help out. At other times, they might say, "I am too busy. I am working on six other things." Sometimes I'll just have to make a decision and say, "Well, let me help you understand why this project is the priority right now. Tomorrow, we can get back to the regular to-do list, but this task really needs attention now."

There's a tendency to take work back, thinking that you'd rather do it yourself than try to clean up the mess when someone makes a mistake. However, this indicates that more time needs to be invested on the front end in making sure that the employee understands everything that is involved and has enough time to do the project properly.

Elizabeth

I'm a big fan of delegation. In my job as CEO, I deal with things that are very strategic and that depend on the long-term vision of the company. Obviously, I'm going to have a better long-term vision of my own company than somebody whom I can bring in and hire by the hour. In essence, I delegate as much as possible. For instance, if I need some writing to get done, and I can find people who are better writers or proofreaders, then I will give those tasks to them. Ideally, I delegate it to the person who will find the task most fun. I also delegate to people's strengths and passions.

When I worked at a consulting firm, I had two people working under me. One was a guy from Caltech, and the other was a guy from UCLA; I delegated fairly between them. I didn't stick them with the unpleasant tasks. I actually looked to see what each needed to learn, and I assigned the tasks that I thought would make each of them grow the most. Even in my own company, the tasks that I can delegate out are sometimes the very worst tasks. In these cases, I end up just doing those tasks myself because I don't want to demoralize anybody else in the process. I just delegate out what needs to be done and what I think will be the next step in their careers, and they are excited about that.

I think the hardest people to manage are volunteers, because volunteers aren't getting paid. When I took over the Red Cross Disaster

Action Team, everybody had been there for years and was just so burned out, so I recruited a lot of new people. Still, there was a lady who was in charge of training, and she was just tired of it. I found a new person who had no training background, but what she really wanted to do in the next step of her career was something in the human resources department at a non-profit organization. I said to her, "Why don't you be in charge of our training, and the lady who used to be in charge of training can mentor you?" The new person was very excited. Instead of using someone who was tired of doing the same task that they already had expertise in, I got a person who *wanted* to do the task and had the person with expertise mentor her. A new person who *wants* to do it has a lot of energy and will bring in new ideas. The new volunteer ended up doing the task really well and then put it on her resume. Interestingly enough, this woman actually did use the experience to her advantage and ended up getting a job with one of the best non-profits in Los Angeles, working in human resources. So, if you take an employee's dreams and connect them to a task, that employee will not only realize his or her own dreams, but will be really excited about the role and will do a great job for you.

The panel agrees that in order to be a good leader you have to delegate. Delegation allows people on your team to grow, which ultimately makes them happier. The leader who holds onto too much of the workload can become overworked and resentful, and that is not nice to anyone. Still, delegation is tricky. You should know what tasks need to be delegated and the proper people to delegate those tasks to. Melanie makes the point that sometimes one must resort to trial and error. You have to see someone's potential first; then, you work with the individual. As Lane puts it, you have to ease people into their respective roles so as not to overwhelm them. Melanie makes the point that the task should be something that excites and challenges the person to grow. Elizabeth shares a wonderful story where she had a person who was burned out as a trainer coach another person who was interested in the trainer position and who was excited about the challenge. She makes the point that it is usually a win-win situation in these circumstances, and she was right, since the apprentice was able to take her experience and turn it into a great career move. Elizabeth not only functioned as a compassionate and effective leader by recognizing that one volunteer was burned out, but she noticed that the new person wanted the opportunity. As a result, the whole process was highly effective for the group.

In Alma's case, working at a small non-profit, she asked for volunteers to take on tasks, so the people who actually wanted to would take them on. This is a nicer approach than just commanding someone to do something and more effective because you usually get a more enthusiastic individual who will naturally do a better job than someone who is doing a task out of obligation. Of course, occasionally Alma did have to kindly explain to her staff why a task was important, if no one volunteered. A kind and effective leader will then guide her team along the way. She will make sure everyone has a clear picture of the end result and break it all into steps. Then, like a compassionate teacher, she will let it go and let the team members do their respective jobs. Jennifer makes the point that you have to trust people to do their jobs, but then check back occasionally to see if everything is headed in the right direction.

Delegation is a wonderful way to guide and train people in order to bring out their true potential. If handled properly, delegation can help people become more excited about their jobs, leading to a very positive and productive experience for everyone involved.

CONTROL

As a leader, you should be in control, but not be too controlling. What kinds of experience have you had with this issue?

Alma

That's a delicate line. You are always kind of tripping around it. I believe women have a different leadership style, or at least some women do, than men. Women tend to be more indirect, for example, asking people for help rather than telling them what is needed.

I don't think anybody would say I'm a micromanager. They would probably say that I should manage more because I come from a place of, "Do your work, so I can do mine." Since my work is also their work, I have to put some time aside to think about what they really need from me. What I really like is strategizing with people, looking ahead and being creative about how we do our work. I think that my most successful working relationships involve more collaboration than control.

Melanie

Instead of a hierarchy, the Girl Scouts is structured as more of a matrix system, so that you're working in teams. For example, I have a staff of seven people, and we interface with other teams. I don't have a top-down feeling with my staff, although I'm responsible. Ultimately, I'm the one whom they have to report to. I am the person responsible for the work and I have to achieve certain goals. I never think, "You work for me, so I'm better than you." We all have our roles, and I'm responsible for many things. At the same time, others have their roles, and I need them as much as they need me. That's always been my perspective.

In terms of control, I never want to micromanage people, but I will rewrite an entire grant proposal if needed. As much as possible, I will get the assigned person to do it. If that person can't do it, then I will just do it myself. I can't do everyone's work, but I won't let things go out that I feel are of lesser   quality. As the leader of my team, I am ultimately responsible for the quality of the work.

Elizabeth

I don't work with people who need to be micromanaged. I prefer people who can be trusted to get their work done without my supervision. I like to keep things flexible and rely on my team's judgment. Occasionally I'll have to step back in if things are significantly off track. I recently had to let someone go who was having trouble making and keeping his own deadlines. I gave him an opportunity to correct the problem, but he didn't. So, I stepped in and took over the job myself until the project was back on track. It's important to be decisive, direct, and firm. A lot of leaders are uncomfortable confronting problems, but if you don't, it wears on the good people on the team.

Lane

I don't think it's as much about control as it's about structure and the methodology of what you're doing. I do think it's very connected to delegation and how well the people on your team know what their jobs entail. Ideally they, in turn, are constantly feeding you information. If you're managing the information properly, then it controls itself. If your staff has been around long enough, you start to get a feel for what works and what doesn't, and that becomes the structure. When the structure is in place, it prevents failures.

For example, if you are a junior producer and you know that you need to hire a designer, then part of the structure is that you have the creative director watch the reel and you talk to the designer about the different projects and so on. You ascertain what strengths this person possesses, and if he or she's the right person to bring on to the project. Part of the structure is reference checking; part of the structure is a weekly resource meeting to discuss hires with the other producers. If there is the right amount of structure, still leaving room for individuality, I find that the success rate soars. Too little, there are mistakes; too much, people feel controlled. It's just a matter of finding the "sweet spot."

Jennifer

You need to allow your staff their space and step in when they need it, either because they're asking for help, or when you see that something maybe going slightly askew. You have to *know* when to step in.

Having said that, again, I have an issue with being a bit of a control freak. I definitely have to try to watch myself so I don't micromanage. I've had bosses who micromanaged me, and I did not like it. So, I try to respect my staff and not do it to them. I think that I have become so busy, though, that I'm not micromanaging these days, and that's a good thing.

The art of control is like the art of delegation. A good leader has to know when to step in and take control. Knowing the right times can be tricky. You have no time to be a leader if you are always checking in with your staff or micromanaging everyone's performance. Micromanaging also implies a lack of trust of your staff. The staff will not be productive, let alone inspired, if they feel that they are not being trusted. The whole panel agrees that the kindest and most effective way to lead in this situation is not to micromanage.

The question then becomes how do you stay in control while not micromanaging? As the panel makes clear, you have to check in once in a while with your staff, but allow them to accomplish each step on their own. Jennifer shares that it is about giving people their space. For Lane, it is not a question of control, but of structure. The structure she uses suggests that everyone is feeding her information so she can keep the project in line. Her team becomes part of the process, and they are involved; she does not have to look over anyone's shoulders. The structure prevents failures, and, if all the team members are doing their jobs, it works. For Alma, she prefers to let people do their jobs and use collaboration rather than control. By strategizing with others, Alma allows everyone to get involved and become part of the process.

Working from a matrix standpoint, Melanie trusts that everyone on her team has their roles and are doing their jobs.

At the end of the day, the buck stops with the leader. The leader is responsible for her team. Again, it's tricky, since a leader has to trust that everyone on her staff is doing his or her job. But what if they're not? Elizabeth, as the CEO of her own company, hires individuals who need no supervision. She still needs to step in and do the job herself if deadlines aren't being met, regardless. That is when a leader must take control. Melanie shares, too, that she will rewrite a grant proposal, if necessary, to assure her organization is properly represented. If done right, a compassionate leader will let her team do their jobs, acting as a guide and checking in once in a while, with the knowledge that she is ultimately responsible for the whole team.

In conclusion, in terms of delegation, lots of it, when possible, is a good thing. Meanwhile, control is necessary, but too much control (micromanaging) shows a lack of trust in your team. All in all, both delegation and control can be quite the balancing act, and a good leader is always aware and conscious of that fact.

CHAPTER 10

Keeping Cool under Pressure

It's a lot easier to be a nice boss when everything is going smoothly, but when pressures or intense deadlines arise, being nice is often the first attribute to go. At these times, bad leaders will lose their cool and sometimes rage at their staff because of their own fears and insecurities. Compassionate and effective leaders, on the other hand, will know how to confidently handle any crisis while keeping their cool. The panel shares their views and methods during such stressful situations.

Many leaders mean well in the beginning, but when pressure comes from upper management or clients, tempers flare. How do you keep your cool? How do you keep your team cool and focused under pressure?

Jennifer

I try to understand where exactly the pressure is coming from instead of just reacting or taking it personally. I try to explain to my team why the situation is so important and high-pressure and I let them know that we are in it together. No one is going to point any fingers at them if something goes wrong.

Again, motherhood has taught me that the crises at work aren't real compared to the ones I have in my family, with a child's illness, for example. There is always a solution, and I always try to convey that to my staff as well.

Lane

I really try hard not to take it personally. It's similar to self-talk. I care about the project, but the project is something separate from me. It's not about me, but it's about how can we all do what's best for the project. Thinking like that helps me take a lot of flack and not respond negatively. Every now and then stuff gets to the best of us, but I don't take it personally.

As for keeping my staff cool, I try to focus on the outcome and on the various solutions. It is important to have a creative response to pressure and think outside the immediate scenario. It's important to trust the process and know that everything that happens, happens for a reason. It will make the outcome more in line with your goal.

Melanie

Staying on top of the workload so things don't get in the pressure cooker is very important. At the same time, I think true leadership is something you live and something you role model. It's under pressure that true leadership is revealed.

Each person on my team is also a leader in her own right. I don't feel like I am the leader—"Hey, look at me!"—or expect them to just defer to me in some way. I empower them in terms of their jobs and their responsibilities and their accountabilities; in that sense, I expect them to lead within their arena. I would also trust them to handle the pressures of the job in their own way and guide them when necessary.

Elizabeth

I try to keep things positive and healthy. I prefer not to make people work crazy hours or use industrial age motivational techniques that revolve around fear and unrealistic deadlines. When there is a real deadline, though, we plan for it in advance and chip away at it. I try to *help* the team rather than cause them extra stress. I take my emotions out of the picture entirely. It's better to treat the team respectfully and constructively and later vent any anger or frustration in private, in my own way, by exercising or painting. Very early on, I lost my temper with an attorney who had done nothing wrong. I had misunderstood him, but I was already feeling angry that day and had not gotten enough sleep the night before. I realized my mistake, apologized to him, and from that situation I learned to pause before reacting emotionally. No matter what happens, you have to remember that disrespect and stinging criticism are very poor ways to manage long-term relationships. It's much better to focus on the outcome that you want rather than on the obstacles.

Alma

We've lost some funding opportunities because of deadlines that we missed or mistakes in not understanding all of the requirements. What do you do? Well, you acknowledge that everybody makes mistakes. If this opportunity doesn't work out, then something else will. I have some personal techniques that are good in defusing situations, and people know that they can depend on me not to panic. I think that's important. If leaders are high-strung and constantly on edge, it's really hard for the rest of the staff to maintain an even temperament and relax enough to do their best work. So, one of my roles is to be that sort of calm, almost methodical, voice of reason, "If we miss this opportunity, we will get another one, but let's try harder next time to get it in on time." I might also analyze the situation and say, "How did we go wrong with this particular project?" Blaming people for mistakes will not typically lead to improvement. If people feel like they are working under threats and pressure, then that's not going to help. It's better to steer out of trouble and keep away from the high drama as much as possible, focusing on areas of improvement. "How can I (or we) help you get this done?" is a question I like to ask. Often the answer can be surprising.

As a leader, it is imperative that you keep calm under pressure. If you get emotional or "lose your cool," you probably won't be very nice, and you certainly will not be effective with your staff. Luckily, the whole panel agrees that you have to stay calm under pressure and role model that behavior at all times during a crisis.

First, as Melanie points out, pressure situations can and should be avoided by staying on top of the workload. Elizabeth offers the insight that it is not good to have people work in fear with unrealistic deadlines. As a leader, when possible, it is important to have realistic deadlines that people can meet. Sometimes, though, a leader might not have control over a deadline due to outside pressures, maybe from a client or customer. In this case, the most compassionate and effective reaction is for a leader to stay calm.

By "staying calm" and taking care of a crisis, the compassionate and effective leader is showing her staff how to stay calm, and she is role modeling how to handle a tense situation. In these instances, Lane does not take the situation personally and employs self-talk to keep calm. Jennifer reminds herself that the crises at work are not like the ones with her children; a solution can always be found. Role modeling calm and confident behavior will put everyone at ease.

The way a leader speaks to her staff during a crisis is important as well. Jennifer, who works within the high-pressure television industry, needs to let her staff know that some situations are high-pressure and that everyone is in it together—no one person is to blame. Alma reminds her staff that everyone makes mistakes and that if deadlines are not met, there will be other opportunities. Melanie continues to empower her staff during a crisis so each person will not feel overwhelmed. Lane and Elizabeth point out that it is good to focus on the outcome and possible solutions when communicating with staff rather than on the obstacles. All of these approaches will help leaders keep their teams calm and on track. Not only are these techniques compassionate, they are effective.

CHAPTER 11

Motivating Your Team through Positive Leadership - Inspiring, Rewarding, and Mentoring

One of the best parts of being a leader at work is that it allows you to offer inspiration to others. Inspiring others will not only make you feel good, but it will motivate your team to do a better job. That better job will have a snowball effect and will lead to another wonderful benefit of being a leader — rewarding members of your team. Finally, finding those individuals who exhibit special talents is a call for mentorship. The panel shares their thoughts on these fulfilling aspects of leadership.

INSPIRATION

How do you inspire your team to do their best?

Jennifer

I try to compliment them on a job well done as much as possible. More importantly, I try to make sure they are always working on projects they really love, enjoy, or make them proud.

With the repetitive nature of television work, it helps to keep things mixed up for them. If they're working on the same show over and over again, responsibilities have to change. Team members have to grow. If you're in development and you've been working on one particular project, you need to keep people feeling that they're working on something they're passionate about. It's also allowing them to work on ideas of their own that might be right for the company. You can't let them go down a road that you know is a dead-end, but if there's potential in someone's idea, you have to encourage it and encourage them to continue to bring in ideas. Let them know that even if their ideas don't always "hit," the fact they are even coming up with ideas is amazing, and one of those ideas will stick one day and will be great. With inspiration, it's just keeping things positive, even when you have to deliver bad news. They have to know that you appreciate what they're doing.

Melanie

I like to role model what I believe is appropriate in the workplace and hope that my example is inspiring. I also tell my staff that if they would like to grow in their positions, hopefully, in the future, there will be opportunities for them to take on. I have one database specialist who just inputs data all day long, and she tells me, "I don't want to do anything else, Melanie. I don't want any pressure. I just want to be able to input," and that's fine. I don't have an expectation that people have to advance. It is not for me; it's for them. Almost everybody that has worked for me has advanced. For example, I hired a woman, who remains a friend, to do marketing communications. She has since left Girls Scouts and was hired by a public relations firm. In the past year, she has had three raises and doubled her salary. She is really capable and she "cut her teeth" by working for Girls Scouts.

Lane

Inspiring your staff is about creating an environment that makes people happy about where they are working. I personally am interested in being fair, objective, and honest with people. I really believe in open communication and treating people well. In the restaurants that I owned, we actually had a very low turnover rate compared to the industry average. At the time, we were doing four times better than the industry as a whole, and I do attribute it to the fact that we were very humane in the way we dealt with our employees, and the employees responded by being positive back to us. It built a sense of teamwork. When you create this sort of atmosphere you gain a lot of employee loyalty, so those hard-to-cover shifts are not a problem. People are *willing* to work when you need them. We also had company parties and picnics each year, so that the employees could get to know each other in a less formal setting. On occasion, I took the key employees — those who I trusted to open or close the restaurant for me, anybody with a supervisory role — out to dinner individually to find out how they were doing. I asked them if they had tips on how we could do things better in the restaurant and if they felt good about their jobs. I think they appreciated the asking, and I always believe that the ones managing and dealing with the public everyday are the ones who really know what's going on. As an owner, I had a good idea of what was going on, but I really needed honest communication from my staff to really create my vision for the restaurant.

Elizabeth

I treat my teammates with love and care, and I see the potential in them. I show them how they can be successful. Most mediocre managers will criticize someone for their weaknesses and try to improve those weaknesses to average. My philosophy is completely the opposite of that. I don't care about your weakness. I can delegate the task to somebody who doesn't have that same weakness. I will tell them, "What I want is for you to focus on your strength and what you are really passionate about and just blossom as a person." I always keep pushing that. People are happier working on their strengths anyway. When you have people working on their strengths, you don't have to motivate them; they are motivated already. The fact that we are working on a project where we are potentially helping people age better over time and the knowledge that 20% of the pre-tax profits are being donated to take clean water, medicine, and supplies to refugee camps and other places around the world that need supplies are big motivators. I don't have to dangle any carrots. My teammates are pretty motivated as they are.

Alma

It's about having passion for the work that we do. If people don't care about art or artists or the creative process, then this is not the right place for them. It's not like we are all cheerleading all the time, but we really invest ourselves in our jobs by trying to go the extra mile and find resources for people. I try to listen to people and demonstrate some personal investment in my staff, and that helps. Inspiration comes when we get excited about the victories, and I try to share all of that as much as possible. We all share the success, the acknowledgment, and the recognition. Our staff often comes to board meetings, and that is really productive. I don't feel like they are just reporting to me. I want them to see and feel that what they do matters and is recognized by the whole organization. We also all get to experience the appreciation from the artists that we help. It's an environment where a lot of people really do understand the links we are making and how we're extending ourselves, and it's all very inspiring.

Inspiring others is one of the most important qualities of a compassionate and highly effective leader. When inspired, a person feels empowered and does her or his best job, and that is good for the person and the company. As Elizabeth and Alma point out, sometimes the work that the company does is inspiring in itself. Then there's the job of a leader to get individuals excited. The panel shares a number of ways to do this. Lane suggests that it all starts with honest communication. Alma suggests a leader should show personal investment in his or her staff. Melanie states that a leader should give people the opportunity to grow. That can be very inspiring. As the owner of restaurants, Lane relied on her managers and would ask for their advice on how to improve certain situations. Her managers would, in turn, feel inspired and empowered and become more invested in the company.

Of course, communication is very important and part of that is to listen to what each team member has to say. When a leader hears what her people need and want, then she is more inclined to see the team members' potentials, as Elizabeth offers. You will then, as Jennifer shares, be able to make sure that your team is working on something they love. As Elizabeth points out, people will feel inspired, as well, when they are working on their strengths and talents. Again, the employee will feel empowered and do a better job. As one of the leaders at a television production company, Jennifer encourages people to work on their own ideas for shows. If the idea does not hit, then she lets the team member know how much she appreciates the effort and creativity.

Appreciation is always inspiring to everyone involved and should be expressed as much as possible. Again, in Jennifer's example, if someone comes up with a great idea, then giving that person credit and public recognition throughout the company is very inspiring to the entire team. Alma agrees that giving public kudos is a good way of inspiring team members. The team will feel empowered and will work harder when they are allowed to shine. Again, it's compassionate and highly effective leadership to make that happen.

Some leaders take all the credit for jobs well done by their staff. Luckily, none of the panelists endorses this notion. "Credit stealing" by a leader is not nice and is counter-productive. The staff will not be inspired, but will feel resentful; they will not feel compelled to do their best job. Alma adds that it helps to get the staff more involved in the company when at all possible. In her job as Executive Director of the California Lawyers for the Arts, Alma invites her staff's participation by inviting them to come to board meetings. Finally, Lane offers that it is also nice to have opportunities for fun once in a while. People spend most of their time at work, and a good leader recognizes that you can work hard and have fun as well. Yes, fun can be inspiring. If people feel joy at work, they are inspired, and that is compassionate and highly effective leadership!

REWARDS

When do you reward a team member, and how do you convey that?

Jennifer

Let's say we sell a show. We'll break out the champagne and share it with the team, and we'll "call people out." I'll say, "Tom, that was amazing. You did this. This is great." I think it's always about sharing. It's always about giving credit where credit is due and making people know that they made it happen. I say that because often I am the one going out and selling a show idea that someone else created. Even though we all developed it together, the person who came up with the idea still needs to get the kudos for it.

Melanie

I convey it very openly and recognize individuals for their accomplishments. I'll say something like: "I think we should all applaud her and treat her to lunch today." I'm very happy to offer words of praise, even if someone is just trying and hasn't really broken through yet or accomplished something. In that situation, I would say, "It is really great that you are trying so hard. I know it is going to fall into place." I try to praise them for their efforts as well as their end result.

Alma

In more prosperous years, we will seek approval from the board of directors to reward the whole team with a modest bonus at the end of the year. At this point, psychological rewards, such as praise and appreciation, are more available than financial ones. We have also sent out group emails congratulating staff members for successful work, and it's great to see that picked up and echoed around the state to people at the different offices. We have a staff e-group where I can post something like, "Wow, Ellen did a great job with the such and such. It's really great to know about the success of the program in Sacramento." Then other people will chime in and congratulate the person and their team. Because we don't get together very often, email communication to the group is one way of reaching everybody and spreading the good news. We also acknowledge staff successes and contributions at meetings of the board of directors.

Elizabeth

I reward people immediately. I don't believe in evaluations that are one year later or even a month later. If someone did something really well, I call that person right away and say, "You did a fantastic job." This last week we had a deadline, and my CTO (Chief Technology

Officer) was brilliant. I told him, "I'm so amazed that you are doing such a fantastic job, even though you don't have very much time in which to do it. I really appreciate your help." You can reward people by just telling them how much you appreciate them and give them time off when they need it. A lot of companies will tell you that they appreciate you, but if someone dies in your family, you only get a week or two off and it doesn't even matter what state you are in. Recently, someone on our team had a family emergency, and I told him just to take as much time off as he needed. Simply respecting people is another way of rewarding them.

Lane

When it comes to individuals, I believe in openly acknowledging a person's great job to everyone. Of course, if a raise is possible, that's always nice to offer, too. You don't want all your rewards to be hierarchical or individual, though. It is important to have some group rewards to help build and develop a team. In one of my recent producer positions, we would occasionally take off on a Friday afternoon and go watch a movie. We would usually watch a movie that had a particularly interesting visual style or effect we wanted to learn more about. It was very heartening to be able to do this research while on the job. It was fun, it was educational, and it was very rewarding for the team to be able to get out of the office and out from behind their computers and just interact and discuss images, stories, and technology.

Whether it is with words or something of monetary value, rewards will guarantee a happy team member, who will seek to continue to do better, and it simply is what compassionate and highly effective leaders do. In order to understand the process of rewarding a member of your team, it helps to know when to reward, how to reward, and what to reward.

*1. **When to reward.** It is always good to reward staff members immediately. If you wait too long, the moment will be lost. It helps to say something immediately if you want the positive behavior to be repeated or happen more often. That might not happen if you wait until evaluation time, as Elizabeth points out.*

*2. **How to reward.** It is usually good to reward people publicly, if possible. Public kudos are very important. Most of the panel share examples of how they reward individuals in front of others. Jennifer's team breaks out the champagne if, say, an idea is sold and toasts the person who came up with the idea. Melanie openly applauds individuals for their achievements and publicly praises individuals for their efforts. Although spreading the word of someone's accomplishment adds to the excitement, Melanie makes the point that a person's sincere efforts are sometimes just as* *praiseworthy. Since Alma is in charge of three different offices, she spreads the good news to all the offices through group email. In addition, Alma acknowledges staff successes and contributions at meetings of the board of directors. Sharing the news throughout the company, especially with high-ranking people, enhances the employee's status and sense of accomplishment.*

In some cases, privacy makes the reward more personal. It is usually better to keep the reward private if it is of monetary value such as gifts and salary increases.

3. What to reward. *Of course, it's always nice to reward someone with a bonus or a raise, depending on both the company's ability to pay and the magnitude of the accomplishment. You don't have to be made of money, though, to be a successful and compassionate leader in terms of rewards. Other options are effective, as well. Giving verbal praise is the most widely used method. Appreciating and respecting the people on your team is also rewarding, as Elizabeth and Melanie point out. Giving people time off when they want it is rewarding them as well, as Elizabeth shares. In addition, Lane offers that group rewards are important. She uses the example of a movie outing as not only fun, but also an opportunity to learn. Again, occasional fun is not only inspiring, it is rewarding.*

MENTORING

Have you mentored anyone now or in the past and what is your process?

Jennifer

My assistant was promoted last year, actually off of my desk. I mentored her, and I tried to include her as much as I could, exposing her to all aspects of production. I knew she was ready to experience all of that, and I knew when she started working for me that she would probably not be my assistant for very long. I was able to keep her for about two years, and that was probably the absolute most that I could have expected. Ultimately, the reason she moved up into a new position at the company is that she is quite talented, but I did mentor her. I was always there, listening and supporting her and trying to help her advance.

Alma

I have served as an informal mentor for several individuals in our organization, both volunteers and staff. The process has involved brainstorming career options, making suggestions about higher education and training opportunities, and being a sounding board when problems arise.

In addition, I am always sharing my knowledge and experience with several staff members, at any given time. Grants are the financial lifeblood of our organization. When we prepare the grant proposals and reports, I work with a lot of different staff members during the various phases of proposal development, such as planning the program, defining the deliverables, and working on the budget and financial reports. There are many opportunities for contact with staff in that particular process that one could see as either delegation or training or mentoring. It's not just about me teaching people, but it's also about listening and trying to understand the opportunities. Then, it's about explaining what our structure is and what our challenges are. During this entire process, a lot of collaborative work is going on in different areas, particularly when we are creating new programs. This kind of mentoring is more informal, but it is fun and rewarding. It also takes a lot of trust and patience.

Lane

I have mentored several younger producers and production managers that I have worked with, not in a formal way, but as a routine part of the job, and I take it very seriously. It is important for young producers to learn how to approach projects from different points of view. This can't be learned by rote, which makes mentoring very important. It is also important that they are able to learn in a slow, structured kind of way, to build on their strengths and not allow the learning process to affect the progress of any particular project. It is a balancing act to offer challenges to someone while continuing to protect the integrity of a project. Mentoring is very rewarding, and I love to see people promoted out from under me.

Melanie

I have had the honor of mentoring several people throughout my career. In every case, the mentee was someone I had hired into a specific position who, despite their many talents, had limited experience in certain arenas. My only approach is hands-on, working with the individual to develop their skills. For example, several years ago, I hired a woman who was an excellent writer, but had no experience in public speaking or fundraising (which the job required). My approach was to work closely with her on general public speaking skills and then bring her with me whenever I had a public speaking engagement with civic organizations or funders. After each speaking engagement, I would ask her what worked and what didn't work in my presentation. In other words, I made her critically assess the strengths and weaknesses of the presentation. After six months of this strategy, I asked her to begin making presentations. She soon became an effective speaker, staying on point with the message, and connecting the audience emotionally to the mission of the organization. In the same way, I worked with her on the basics of fundraising and donation solicitation. Eventually she and her husband moved to another city, but she had become a great asset to me and the organization before she left. She came in as a good writer, but she left as an excellent marketer, communicator, and fundraiser.

Elizabeth

Whenever I speak at business schools, I usually end up with several requests for mentorship. I'm happy to mentor others, but only if they are serious about taking action towards their goals. I usually tell people to contact me in three weeks if they would like me to mentor them. Most people will forget and only the serious ones will send an email reminding me. I talk to them, see what their goals are, see where they are stuck, and offer a little guidance when needed. People generally aren't aware of how powerful they really are, so it's often just a gentle nudge that can change their trajectory for the better.

Nurturing new leaders for the future is what a good leader does. A bad leader will feel threatened by talented people coming up in the ranks; a good leader will be excited about it and will want to groom the next generation of leaders. In addition, the mentee will likely benefit the mentor as well as the company. Elizabeth made this point in Chapter 2, on being a school mentor, that she learned a lot from her mentees.

Not only have the women on this panel had many wonderful mentors, but they are now mentoring the next generation. Each of the panel has their own methods and acts as a kind and compassionate guide. Alma mentors in two different ways. With certain individuals, Alma will discuss and brainstorm higher education and various career opportunities for that person. Otherwise, on a daily basis, her method of mentoring is more casual and informal with a variety of people. She makes sure she is always sharing her knowledge with her staff and helping others by training and/or delegating along the way. Lane routinely trains young producers as part of her job. The mentees do not just learn by rote; she teaches them to approach projects from varying points of view. She does not rush the process, but teaches in a slow and structured way that builds on the mentees' strengths. Using the example of her assistant, Jennifer saw her potential and encouraged it by exposing her to the production process and by listening, supporting, and assisting her in moving up in the company.

Elizabeth employs a more formal method of mentorship. Since Elizabeth speaks at business schools, she gets called on to mentor young people from outside her organization. She discusses the mentees' goals to find out where they may be stuck. She encourages them and reminds them how powerful they are. Elizabeth notices that she just needs to give a gentle nudge to get a mentee on track to where he or she needs to go.

Finally, Melanie's story shows what compassionate and effective mentorship looks like in action. Melanie's hands-on method while training a mentee is very interactive. She uses the example of training a woman on her team how to speak effectively and fundraise. She taught her, then showed her. While doing this, Melanie actually asked the mentee to critically assess her (Melanie's) own strengths and weaknesses, in order to allow the mentee to participate in the process. That is truly humble! An ego-driven leader would never allow such a thing. Melanie guided her mentee through the entire process, until her mentee became very successful at speaking, marketing, and fundraising. She achieved this mostly by being a great role model. Melanie also makes the point that her mentee became a great asset to her and the company. Mentorship is not only compassionate, it is truly beneficial to all involved.

CHAPTER 12

Dealing with the Negative Aspects of Leadership – Poor Performance, Conflicts, and the Firing Process

Probably the most challenging part of leadership is delivering bad news to individual team members. I refer to those difficult conversations about bad job performance and bad behavior between team members, as well as the most-dreaded conversation of all — when you have to say, "You're fired," to a member of your team. The panel shares how they handle each of these difficult conversations with fairness and compassion, in a way that allows all involved to walk away a little more enlightened, even in the worst-case scenarios.

POOR PERFORMANCE

When a team member does a poor job, how do you let them know?

Alma

It has to be through some sort of self-evaluation. If people recognize that they messed up or they didn't hit the target, it's more of a one-on-one conversation about how the situation happened and how to avoid it in the future. I simply ask them, "What can we do differently next time? What kind of support do you need?"

Lane

It depends on how serious it is. If it's minor enough and I happen to be in a group, I can say, "Okay, what you could do next time is such and such." It can be very casual, and everyone can learn from it. If it's really serious, I want to discuss it in private and as quickly as possible. So, it really depends on how major the screw-up is, whether it should be handled publicly or privately.

Melanie

I just talk with them very directly. I also set benchmarks to check and see if we are falling behind with projects or monies raised. I do understand that there is a learning curve, and I try to work with individuals so they will learn if mistakes do happen. In certain cases, I've had to let people go whose work was inferior. Usually, I find that the person wasn't really happy in the position anyway.

Elizabeth

If a teammate is doing something wrong and needs to be guided, it's important to say, "That's a good try." Then, show that person a better way to accomplish the task. You also have to show him or her instantly, rather than, let's say, three weeks later. If you say something after too much time has gone by, the teammate may not remember the situation clearly, and you may sound petty.

Jennifer

If someone on your staff does a poor job, you should meet with that person and talk about what can be done differently the next time. You always have to keep it positive because you don't want employees leaving your office feeling bad. They have to leave your office wanting to do better.

The most compassionate way to deal with someone's poor performance is to actually deal with it directly. Otherwise, you are setting the person in question up to fail again and again, and that is not "nice" for anyone – either for the individual or for the rest of the team.

Of course, how you deal with the situation is important, too. The panel shows that it is actually more effective to be sensitive and understanding. Overall, the panel agrees that the following four points are important considerations when confronting negative performance issues with a team member:

1. Timing. Let the person know immediately, as soon as possible, after the incident in question. This way the person can correct the problem right away. If it is too late, you need to show them how they can improve the next time. Also, as Elizabeth points out, if you wait too long to tell the person about his or her poor job performance, it will sound petty.

2. Objectivity. *It is important to be as objective as possible in order to keep the criticism from becoming too personal. Without avoiding the individual's personal responsibility, keep the discussion about the needs of the organization and the proper role of each participant generally.*

When correcting behavior, it has to be about the task at hand and not the person. Elizabeth makes the point that the nicest way to deal with the poor performance is to be direct with the person. From there, it is time to help that person and give the necessary guidance so the person can do a better job next time. In addition, Jennifer states that it is important to keep the talk on a positive note so the person will feel good and want to improve his or her job performance.

3. Solicit the individual's opinion. *Involve the person in the discussion, allowing her to suggest her own ideas for a solution. Letting the person contribute to the discussion avoids a "top-down" approach and the corresponding feelings of fear and intimidation. These negative feelings only lead to resentment and resistance to an effective solution.*

A very effective way to include the team member's opinion is to allow that person to "self-evaluate." For instance, Alma suggests using questions like, "What can we do differently next time?" It implies that you are with the person and working together to do a great job. Lane also recommends self-evaluation and then offering suggestions and showing the team member a better way.

4. Privacy. Depending on the gravity of the situation, giving the individual the respect and consideration of a private discussion will avoid embarrassment and a compounding of problems down the road.

Lane makes the point that if it is something minor, it can be shared with the group so everyone can learn. If it is major, it is wise and kind to talk to the person in private to avoid embarrassment.

Using these methods for dealing with a team member's failing performance creates a win-win situation for everyone involved.

CONFLICTS

How do you deal with personal conflicts within your team?

Lane

You have to be a mediator. When working as a producer, I have different designers working on projects. They usually have differing opinions about how things should work. I solve problems by talking them through calmly. It is helpful to bring everybody together, and it can be very informal. You discuss what each person really thinks and how he or she would solve the problem. Then, you discuss criteria, and eventually you reach an understanding or a resolution. Luckily, there are no fights. It's all dialogue.

In the restaurant business, there were definitely conflicts, because the wait staff's job is dealing with the public, and the servers are under a lot of stress. I could feel the tension in my employees. If it felt like something that needed to be diffused, even if it hadn't been verbalized yet, I would try to diffuse it before a conflict broke out. If something already had broken out, like a remark had been made, I would guide individuals into a private space in order for them to talk it over without others listening. This way the employee felt safe. In any business, these are the kinds of decisions that have to be made, often on the spur of the moment.

Melanie

I try to work with each person individually. Recently, I had a situation where one worker was very dismissive towards another; even though deferential towards me. I had to speak with her very directly. Of course, she has her own personality, but I needed to make it clear that her behavior was not acceptable. It's not *what* she was expressing but *how* she was expressing it. I could not brush it under the rug, because I didn't want it to come up in the future. I want there to be a feeling of mutual respect and support among team members, and they need to bring that to the table. I bring those qualities to the table, and I expect everyone else to do so with each other. In an organization as large and well established as the Girls Scouts, there is the human resources element of reports on people's performance. I am not someone who will look to report people, but if the employee can't correct the behavior, then it will be necessary for me to write it up.

Elizabeth

How do I deal with personal conflicts within the team? I tell them to grow up. Often when the team has a new member, somebody will start a "pecking order" war, and I will say, "Listen, you two aren't kids. You were both hired because you are experts. You have expertise in your area, and you have expertise in yours, and you need to get along. If you can't, I'm going to get rid of you — end of story." There's no time for any of that. I don't see work as a place where it's okay to bring that stuff in. You are hired to do a job. If you don't like someone on the team, get to know the person better; you might find that you like him or her. If you can't like the person, then keep it to yourself. As for being grumpy, I leave that stuff at the door, and I expect everybody else to do the same. It can turn into a toxic environment very easily if somebody is frustrated and takes it out on somebody else. That is just not okay. I think a lot of workplaces tolerate that too much, and once you let one person do it, it becomes, "Well, if that one person can have a lack of emotional intelligence, so can I." Or maybe the team member thinks, "I can't go to that place, because I'm lower in rank," and the power differentials start to come into play. I just let them know we are all equal, we are all humans, and we need to treat each other with respect. If they can't do that, they need to go home.

Jennifer

I had a situation arise in the recent past. I spoke to each person separately and asked them to try and work it out. I tried to explain to each of them where the other one was coming from, to soften the edges a little bit, and then I encouraged them to talk to each other to see if they could work it out. You can't ignore a problem completely because it may never go away. There may come a point when it becomes a big issue, and something must be done about it, when it may be necessary to move one or both of them to other teams. It just depends on the situation, but I have been in the middle of it and found it important not to blame one over the other. You just have to try to get each of them to see the situation through the other's eyes; sometimes it works, and sometimes it doesn't.

Alma

Something came up recently where two people were complaining about each other, and I spoke to each of them. I said, "Would it be helpful for the three of us to have a conversation about this?" They each said, "Sure." I then heard quite a lot from each of them about what was going on, and I made some suggestions. The main issues involved communication styles. I knew more than either of them about the work that the other was doing. I requested that each of them have empathy for the other and to understand each other's deadlines and pressures. I said, "You need to understand what this person is doing and all the things on her plate and also try to understand how she wants you to communicate with her." About a week later, I checked in with both of them again and asked how things were going. Both parties told me the situation had gotten a lot better. I said, "Well, that's good. I don't think we need that meeting" and they agreed. They were able to work it out using their own insight.

I think certain work situations are not going to be perfect because people are different. Some people really like long verbal explanations; others just want written memos. It gets down to how to best communicate with all the different people you work with, to know them and understand the best way for them to hear you. We all start out with the idea of everyone wanting to do the best we can for the community we serve, and it's good to nurture a common understanding of what we are doing. It's in the best interest of the organization, and it's a better way to start out in any work relationship.

I try not to get emotionally involved in my employees' conflicts because that wouldn't be helpful. Nor do I want to take sides. I want people to assume responsibility for bridging those gaps with each other; a facilitative approach can help.

Personal conflicts should not exist in anyone's workplace, but they do. Again, as a leader, the "nicest" thing you can do for everyone is to deal with it. Otherwise, the conflict may blow up and become a bigger problem.

The panel's advice on this issue of conflicts between people is similar to their advice regarding poor performance from individuals, keeping the same four points in mind:

*1. **Timing.** It is very important to take care of conflicts as soon as they arise. Lane remembers feeling the tensions among her restaurant employees and understanding how important it was to diffuse a situation as quickly as possible. For instance, if a remark was made, she had to deal with the situation on the spur of the moment.*

*2. **Privacy.** Whenever possible, it is wise to speak first to each person involved in a conflict privately to get his or her point of view. While* *managing restaurants, though, Lane did not always have time to talk to each person separately. She would instead take the two people in question to a private space and try to resolve the problem as quickly as possible. Respecting your employees' privacy in these situations is always good policy; your employees will appreciate this.*

3. Objectivity. To truly understand a conflict between two people, it is important to be objective. Lane acts as a compassionate mediator by talking through the problem with both people in a calm and rationale manner until there is resolution. As Jennifer and Alma suggest, you cannot take sides. You have to understand the situation from each person's point of view.

4. Solicit the individuals' opinions. As most agree, you should give the people involved the responsibility and allow them the opportunity to bridge the gap between them. Lane offers that one should discuss with each person separately what he or she really thinks about the situation and how to solve the problem. Jennifer and Alma suggest that part of the mediation process is getting each party to understand the other's perspective and the pressures the other is facing in an effort to create empathy. Also, finding an area of agreement between the parties will help lead them to a solution. Finding common ground will also help in terms of empathy. Of course, the most effective and beneficial common ground is the two wanting what is best for the company.

If conflicts still continue, there other routes. Melanie does try to work with people first, but if people do not improve, then she will report the problem to the human resources department. This may seem unkind, but Melanie uses this as a last resort after her requests for individual improvement have failed. Jennifer has the option of moving people away from each other to work on other shows. Elizabeth has a slightly different tact. She has her own company and knows the people fairly well; she believes she can talk directly to them and say, "Grow up." This tact may be perceived as a bit harsh, but it is being direct and requesting mutual respect, which is nice to everyone.

Allowing employees to treat each other with disrespect creates a toxic environment. People cannot do their best jobs in such situations. Again, kindness and mutual respect create an environment where everyone can work in harmony and do the best job possible.

THE FIRING PROCESS

When do you let a team member go? What chance do you give a team member to improve before letting him or her go?

Lane

When I owned restaurants, if a staff member was not doing her job properly, we always went through a three-step process. First, we talked to her about it, so she understood that she did something wrong and needed to fix it, and we gave her a time limit. If that didn't solve the problem, the second step was to put it in writing, because sometimes it is difficult for an employee to "get it" unless you have it written down on paper. I would write an explanation of what needed to be improved and made sure the employee understood it, then we both would sign it. I would also make sure that she understood that if it was not corrected, she would be let go, which was the third step.

In the creative business, you can let people go for creative differences at any time. If people have differing points of view on creative projects, that's just the way it is. Still, I don't want anybody to be let go and have it be a surprise, because I want to be thoughtful in the way that I deal with people. I want to be gentle with people about the fact that they're going to be without an income. It's best to let people know upfront that they're going to be let go if they don't take care of the problems at hand.

For me, firing people is never pleasant; it's always uncomfortable. If you make it as clear as possible beforehand, it helps pave the way for a smoother process.

Alma

Over the years, I haven't had to terminate very many people. I'm so glad because it's a horrible thing. When I do need to fire an employee, though, I call on Jack Davis, a wonderful labor lawyer who sits on our organization's board of directors, and heads our Personnel Committee. He usually suggests that I review the personnel policy with regard to termination in order to make sure there is no discrimination, and that appropriate warnings have been given. Of course, if an employee has committed an egregious act, like theft or assault, it is grounds for immediate termination. Otherwise, it is best to come to an understanding that things are not working well. It is usually mutually obvious, though, when it's not working out.

Melanie

I go to tremendous lengths to fix the problem before I let someone go. I don't feel people are expendable, and I do think there's a learning curve. It's strange that in all the jobs I've had, I've never been prepared for them. I've always been thrown into situations that were either left in shambles or didn't exist in the first place, and I've had to build them from scratch. At first, I would be somewhat overwhelmed, and I would work crazy hours trying to organize things. So, I'm sympathetic to individuals who are put in those kinds of situations.

I've made two really bad hiring decisions, which I've learned from. They were both very hard for me because I go to great lengths not to demean anyone, but things don't always work out. Some people are not right for the job, and, as time goes on, their weaknesses become very apparent. Other people really promote themselves or sell themselves in an interview, but turn out to be less qualified than expected. Resumes account for something, but honestly not for everything. It is hard to let people go because they have lives and families, and I take this into account. However, if a person is doing damage to the organization, then I have to make that decision.

Elizabeth

If there has been a massive integrity breach, then I will immediately terminate the person involved. Otherwise, I give people sufficient guidance before letting them go. However, once I have made the decision to terminate a teammate, I am straightforward and say, "I need to let you go because of this, this, and this." Many people in business will tell you not to let the teammate know why you are letting him or her go, because it might be lawsuit fodder. I personally think it's important to treat people the way you want to be treated and be direct with them. If I was being fired, I would want to know why, and I would want to know that I was fairly evaluated in the process.

When I was very young, I had my own graphic design company, and I did end up firing people quite often. I would hire people, and they would end up being on drugs or otherwise unreliable. When they would miss their first deadline, I would go see what the problem was, and I might give them another chance. If it was obvious that this person was problematic, I would just take them off the project and put somebody else on. By trial and error I developed a model for hiring, so I would not find myself in the situation of firing designers so often. I started having prospective candidates work as independent contractors on one or two projects before hiring them. This way I could know what it was like to work with them. Do they meet their deadlines? Are they pleasant to work with? Are they honest? If they don't meet that criteria, then I don't have to hire them, which means I don't have to fire them. It's that simple.

Jennifer

I think I know in my gut early on when someone isn't going to work out. It's not fair, though, to make a snap decision about letting someone go. I usually give people a chance. I try to talk to them and try to guide them before I make the decision to let them go. You should have a couple of talks with people before you get to that point where you feel like, "Okay, that's it!" And I don't think the talks necessarily have to be, "Listen, I'm ready to fire you, and you have to prove to me that I shouldn't fire you," because I feel that puts someone in a really bad position, and a person might have a tough time recovering after such a talk. You have to try to give people constructive criticism and just see what happens, see whether or not they are able to make it work.

Ultimately, if someone is not right for the job, you can't just keep the employee around because you feel guilty about it. It does the company a disservice, and I don't think it does the employee any good either. So, if I have to let someone go, I usually try to figure out how to do it in the most humane way possible. I also want to be supportive. Sometimes an employee hasn't done anything specifically wrong. The job just might not be right for him or her. I try to focus on the strengths that the employee does have and guide him or her towards maybe looking for a job in a slightly different area. I work in a production company, so there are lots of jobs on shows where someone may be better suited verses being in an office job. There are different alternatives, but I also don't believe in moving someone around to a different department if I don't think he or she is going to thrive there either. I think that happens a lot, where management pushes someone off on another department and lets the other department deal with the problem. I think that's a mistake, but I do believe if someone's good and tries hard, it's important to try to find that person another placement within the company. If it's not possible, then you support the employee when he or she leaves. You help the employee out, too, if he or she asks for the help.

I also think it's important to not lie about someone's strengths or weaknesses if another employer calls and asks you. You should be very careful about what you say. At the same time, you have to make sure that you are telling the truth and not hurting the former employee's chances in any way. In other words, you can give someone the truth and focus on the positives and say, "This is what this person is good at," or "It wasn't my experience that was one of this person's strengths, but this trait certainly was." You have to choose your answers carefully so that the person is able to find work again.

The whole panel agrees that firing someone is an unpleasant, but sometimes necessary, experience. It may seem like the nicest thing to do is let someone stay in his or her job, but as Melanie suggests it is not good to keep someone who is doing damage to the company. Doing that is not being kind to the company or the other employees. The panel also agrees that a compassionate leader gives the person in question sufficient warnings, guidance, and the opportunity to improve. As with Lane's restaurant protocol and the human resources guidelines set up at many companies, it is a three-step process. First, you tell them about the problem. If they do not improve, you write down the problem in memo form and have them sign it. If the problem persists, you let them go. Companies have varying procedures, but all well-run companies give a person a fair chance. In Alma's situation, she consults with a labor lawyer. Besides giving appropriate warnings, he advises Alma to make sure there is no discrimination involved. Alma says it helps, too, if you can come to a mutual understanding with the employee that the situation is not working for the person or for the company. Sometimes a person is just not happy in the job, and his presence does not help the company or him be very productive.

Jennifer says that when you do fire someone, it must be in the most humane way possible. During the session, you should point out a person's strengths and that he or she may be better suited for a different job. This will empower the person. Also, without lying, it is kind and compassionate to let future employers who may call you know that the person does have strengths and point them out. The person's new job may be a better fit! Of course, firing is immediate and necessary when someone does something egregious (such as theft). Lane and Elizabeth suggest the firing process can be avoided if you can test an employee's performance first by hiring the individual as an independent contractor or on a conditional basis. The person and the company will see if they are a good fit for each other. This is a nice and effective method for all involved.

CHAPTER 13

Being Nice Without
Being a Pushover

I believe a lot of people really do want to be nice as a leader, but they either haven't had a good role model showing them how to do that while still being effective, or they don't trust that their team won't take advantage of them if they do show kindness. The panel shares their thoughts on how to be nice without being a pushover.

How do you manage to be nice without your team taking advantage of you?

Jennifer

I'm nice, but I'm not a pushover. If someone treats me in a way that I'm not happy with, I am not afraid to tell them. To me, being nice and being a pushover are two different things. I think people perceive me as nice and may underestimate me at times, but no one has taken advantage of that to my knowledge, and I wouldn't let them, anyway.

Lane

I do it with boundaries. I set conditions. For instance, I may say, "If you give me your request in by such and such a time, then I will do XYZ for you." It's very structured. I don't play favorites, so people can't take advantage of me. I protect myself from that kind of behavior. Thank goodness, or else it could get vicious. I think being nice is always important, but you can be nice and still keep your boundaries.

Melanie

As a boss, I think there are certain boundaries. I am not the taskmaster type. While I have a high expectation of the people that are on my team, I have a higher expectation for myself. I am not going to simply push papers; that is not for me. I am trying to achieve something and create revenue streams so we can deliver programs to thousands of girls, many of them in underserved communities who cannot afford it. There is a real mission to the work. For this reason, if I feel that I am being taken advantage of, I speak up about it.

I usually try to accommodate people with difficult circumstances, as long as they can keep up with the work. I want to be considerate of people's family situations or health situations. One of my team members volunteers to conduct a grief workshop for parents once a week, so she needs to leave work early on that day. Of course, she can leave work early. It's not an issue for me. That is part of her contribution to her community, and it is for her own life. I think I'm just as direct with the people who work "under me" as I am with the CEO and the people that work "above me." I've developed a strong identity, and I feel respect for everyone equally.

Elizabeth

I don't tolerate people who take advantage of kindness. The people that view kindness as a weakness are fundamentally less evolved, so it's better to just get away from them as fast as possible. In these instances, I can become someone I'm not and become very guarded in order to make sure this person is not going to take advantage of me. I would rather just let the person go so I can be "my kind self" and be around people who respect that and are okay with that. Not everyone can respect kindness; it really comes down to your upbringing and your values.

Alma

We have a very liberal personnel policy which allows paid sick leave when genuinely needed. We don't have a strict limit on sick days allowed, and we don't ask for medical verification forms. If you really need to be out because you are sick, then we just assume that's truly the case. I don't know if the policy is abused, but it easily could be. I don't have any tools or desire to find out. Maybe some people are taking advantage of it, but it is marginal, and it isn't worth it to me to worry about it. Leading by example is the key. I feel that if I never lie about being sick it solves 50% of the problem. If I lie about it, everybody will. My solution is not to take advantage of the system myself, and I try to give 110%. Then I don't mind asking other people to work a little extra when it's needed. It is fruitless to worry about people taking advantage. It's a needless negative vibe.

I worked at a job for about five months where they were very busy worrying about me taking advantage. They weren't concerned about the quality of my work; they were just concerned about the time I came in every morning, after initially saying that I could work a flexible schedule. I was working as a lawyer, and the company wanted me there at the same exact time every day. It didn't matter that I worked late into the night or that my work was very individuated. I finally left because the situation had become so demoralizing. If you worry about people taking advantage, you're basically saying that you don't trust them. It does not create a healthy work environment.

Being "nice" has really gotten a bad reputation in business leadership. The word "nice" has been associated with being weak and letting employees figuratively walk all over you. Jennifer makes a good point – being nice and being a pushover are two different things. The panel discusses in previous chapters how to be nice in order to produce the most effective results. For example, Melanie offers that being nice is developing a mutual respect between her and her staff. She also gives an example of being nice as trying to accommodate reasonable requests from her staff. Being nice in these regards is about being fair and treating everyone equally.

If you do think people might take advantage, what should you do? Jennifer and Melanie make the point that if people are taking advantage of them, they stand up for themselves. This implies talking directly with someone in private, as mentioned in the previous chapter about dealing with conflicts between people. Many on the panel believe that people will not take advantage if you use boundaries. For example, Lane sets boundaries by not playing favorites. She also sets up structured rules, such as, if you meet the requirements you can be granted time off. This fair play is effective and productive. No one will feel slighted. On the other hand, by playing favorites, for example, resentment may set in with employees who are not getting the same special treatment.

As CEO of her own company, Elizabeth does not tolerate anyone taking advantage of her kindness. She would prefer to let someone go rather than have to change her "kind" personality. Of course, firing someone may not be so nice, but it is nicer than letting the person's negativity weigh down the environment or make her a guarded person. This isn't good for anyone. By sending an employee home for the day because of his grumpiness, for example, Elizabeth is actually being compassionate to everyone else by not letting the work environment become toxic.

On the other hand, Alma makes the point that if you worry about people taking advantage, you really are sending out the wrong signal to your employees. You are saying to your employees that you don't trust them. She shares her own story of how she worked hard for another company that was always worried about her taking advantage. Alma found the experience extremely demoralizing. Since she knows what a negative effect it had on her, she knows that would not be a good situation for her own staff. To trust people and give them the benefit of the doubt makes for a lot healthier work environment. It is kind, and it makes it easier for people to do their best work.

It seems that you can find a balance between being firm and being too controlling. Each leader must find his or her own balance by being sensitive to the needs of individuals, his or her own personal needs, and the needs of the group. Hopefully, some of the examples given by the panel suggest to you ways of striking the right balance in different situations.

Ultimately, the best way to prevent people from taking advantage, as Alma states, is to lead by example. If you don't take advantage, then chances are your staff won't either. Being a great role model that goes the extra mile for your staff will make others go the extra mile for you. It is compassionate leadership, and it is extremely productive.

CHAPTER 14

Being Friends with Employees –
Is it Possible?

Being a nice leader does not mean you have to be friends with your team. There will be occasions, though, when you may want to be friends with some members of your staff. Again, I asked the panel how they handle the issue of being friends with their employees.

Have you been friends with employees? Is this a good idea or not?

Jennifer

Yes, I have been friends with my employees, but there's still a line there. Luckily, I haven't had a problem with it. My staff respects my boundaries enough. I don't go out and party with people that work for me, but we do socialize on occasions such as office Christmas parties or other special events. On these occasions we have fun socially, but I have my own personal life that's very separate from work. That, in itself, prevents that line being crossed too much. I have kids, and I'm older. Most of my employees have a different lifestyle. I think, though, it's good to let your employees know a little bit about you. It's okay to share personal stories on both sides as long as it doesn't get *too* personal. You don't want to tell them too much, but it's okay to show them that, even as the boss, you're not all business.

Lane

I don't think it's a good idea to be friends with your employees. I'm always friendly and warm, but being friends creates a conflict of interest and makes it really tough on you as a leader. I've known people who have been friends with their employees, and it doesn't always work out.

Having said that, the entertainment business seems to be much more friend-oriented than the restaurant business. In production, there are a lot of "Mom and Pop" production companies and relationships seem to mesh between the professional and the personal. For instance, the husband may be the director, and the wife may be the producer. I think, however, that many times being friends or having romantic relationships can create problems with perceived favoritism and can create vulnerabilities. As a leader, I don't want that exposure.

Alma

You don't want to become best friends with the people you're supervising because it becomes difficult when you start having problems. That doesn't rule out becoming friends with some employees, which has happened. For example, I'm still friendly with one of the women who used to run our Los Angeles office.

In general, though, I wouldn't say that I am going out socializing with people I work with very much. It's not a policy thing; I'm just too busy. Sometimes it's challenging keeping it separate, but I feel that the people who work with me would rather have a social life apart from mine. I mean, why would you want to hang out with your boss? It doesn't usually work. You don't want everything you do to be exposed throughout your workplace either. People need boundaries. Nevertheless, I've have had some interesting opportunities to travel with staff for work. Although it would not be considered social life, it provides the opportunity for camaraderie, and that's nice.

Melanie

I think you can be friends with your employees. I had brunch recently with two of my former team members in Girl Scouts. One person I had hired to be the grants manager in the San Fernando Valley and the other person I hired to do marketing and communication. They are both great and they are really powerful women in their own right. They are really fun and interesting as well. One in particular didn't quite fit into the Girl Scouts scene, but we were able to work and have fun together. We're still friends, which is really nice.

Obviously, everyone I have hired or who works with me is not my friend, but I want the people that work with me to be able to have fun, enjoy, learn, grow and build something wonderful together.

Elizabeth

I'm friends with all my teammates, the ones I've hired for my company. Rarely do I hire strangers. One of the founding members of our team is someone I didn't know, but he was a college friend of one of the other founding members. So, somebody has known him for a while. Everybody else I have known for a long time or have worked with before. I don't like working with strangers, or, I should say, I prefer working with friends.

In order to be a compassionate and effective leader, you do not have to be friends with any of your employees. Actually, as most of the panel implies, being friends can be a tricky proposition that may create conflicts. For example, as Lane suggests, being friends with certain employees and not others may imply favoritism. That, in turn, will put others on the staff off and may create an atmosphere of resentment. This is not the atmosphere an effective leader fosters. Also, Alma brings up the point that being too close and too familiar with people may make it more difficult to correct their behaviors if it becomes necessary.

Friendships are possible, but it really depends on the people involved and the work environment. For example, Melanie has been friends with some of the people she has led and seems to have no problem with the notion. This situation might be partly due to the atmosphere of Girl Scouts, where a matrix-style work model is in place, and teams interface equally rather than in a top-down patriarchal style. At Girl Scouts, people who work in these various teams treat each other fairly and equally from the beginning, which may make friendships more possible between team leaders and members. As CEO of her own startup company, Elizabeth hires just her friends whom she knows and trusts and believes can do the job. Elizabeth does not have to worry about someone sabotaging her or taking credit for the job she does, since she is the person in charge. Also, as Lane points out, smaller companies are often started by friends who then build the company together. In larger companies, where the environment and the people are not so easily controlled, issues of favoritism and competition can put friendships in jeopardy.

Being friendly, as the panel agrees, seems to be the preferred method for becoming the most compassionate and effective leader. The difference between being friends and being friendly is making sure boundaries are in place. Jennifer says she is friends with her staff, but only to a point. She does not believe in getting too personal. However, she feels it is acceptable to share some personal things to show you are not all business. In other words, it is okay to show everyone that you are human too. Creating a sense of camaraderie with your staff, as Alma puts it, is nice. You can have good times with your staff through office parties or excursions. The staff does it together, and it is fun. Such a warm and friendly manner makes for a happier work environment, too.

It is important to know, too, that you do not have to be friends with your staff to create an atmosphere, as Melanie states, that is fun and enjoyable, where everyone is creating something wonderful together.

PART III

THE GENDER ISSUE

CHAPTER 15

The Advantages and Disadvantages of Being a Woman in Leadership

Although women have come a long way over the past several years in terms of leadership at work, a lot of inequality still exists. Women still do not hold as many high-end leadership positions in companies and still do not make the same amount of money as their male counterparts. Progress is being made every day, and each generation seems to have it a little easier than the generation before. With this in mind, I asked each member of the panel to offer their opinion in regards to the advantages and disadvantages of being a woman in leadership.

In terms of leadership, what are the advantages and disadvantages of being a woman?

Jennifer

I think women exhibit more compassion in situations. I don't think women make snap decisions. They think things through. Women can go into tense situations in a way that is less threatening than men sometimes do. This is a big plus, that women have a way of being involved without ego. Because of that, I feel people may be a little bit more open with women in intense situations.

As for disadvantages, I don't see many, if any, in terms of leadership for women. There's a boys' club that still exists at times, but it hasn't had a negative impact on me, personally. Fortunately, there are a lot of women executives in the television industry, and I do believe we are helping each other.

Alma

In terms of advantages, I think that women have really refined listening skills and are often more in tune with intuition and emotions than men are. Women are also able to be disarming in certain situations. Having all of these qualities and what I call a "soft focus" really helps in mediation and problem solving, as well as in organizational leadership.

Sometimes expectations are lower for women in leadership positions—which could be a disadvantage—or an opportunity. It's always great to exceed other people's expectations.

Melanie

The advantage women have is also their disadvantage. A good point about women working with women is they listen to everyone's opinion, much more so than men do. A masculine approach is to sometimes use the fear factor of "whatever the boss says is right." I have found that is much less true in women-run organizations. At the same time, the weakness is the process can get stalled, because women are sometimes reluctant to make enemies by making a decision that might seem unpopular. An important element of leadership, though, is that you have to make a decision and then stand by it.

Elizabeth

I actually think that it's better to be a woman in business for lots of reasons. One is that your viewpoint is appreciated because it is different. I just graduated from business school, where it was 70% men, 30% women. I would come up with ideas that the men in my class wouldn't. Biologically, a woman's corpus callosum is thicker than a man's, which means the left and right side of a woman's brain communicates more, so women tend to think more holistically. Studies show that women consider other people's feelings more. Studies also show that companies that have women at the top tend to do better than companies that have no women at the top. Investors who are women tend to out-perform investors of the same caliber who are men. I also think that women stand out more just because they are in the minority. So, I have never felt disadvantaged because I am a woman.

I can't imagine being alive two generations ago and being a woman looking for a job. During the late 1960s, in Michigan, the kinds of questions my mother was asked during job interviews were unbelievable. She was literally asked about her menstrual cycle, if she thought she could handle the job on those days. It's ironic, because she is a gynecologist and was being interviewed for that position. My Mom told the interviewing doctor, "Yes, I can handle the job. Life doesn't stop on those days." They hired three residents, one of whom was my mother, with the understanding that only two of them would be kept at the end of the year. They were sure that they were going to get rid of my Mom, but she turned out to be the hardest worker out of all three, and the doctor who hired them made her a partner within two years. They didn't have many women in the positions of surgeon or obstetrician back then. They had all the stereotypes in their heads, and my mother's generation had to fight against that. That's why I go out of my way to honor the generations above me and thank them for kicking in the doors of sexism and demanding equality.

Lane

Women often bring an intuitiveness, motivation, and relationship-building style to management, and these qualities are to a leader's true advantage in today's work world.

For many years, women have tried to move up the ladder in a traditionally masculine situation or hierarchy. In the past, it was very difficult because women were stereotypically seen as emotional or not able to handle the "man's world." Also, it was hard to break into the culture and camaraderie of an all male domain. I feel that these stereotypes are changing, however, as time goes on. The situation for women has improved, but we still have a way to go.

When I first entered the work force in the 1970s, jobs were listed in the newspaper as either "women's jobs" or "men's jobs." When I got my first job at a restaurant, women weren't allowed to be managers. They didn't say it outright, but they didn't allow women to be cooks, and only cooks could become managers! Luckily, a few of the male cooks trained me on my own, unpaid time. One night they needed a cook, and I was the only one available; I cooked, and they finally had to pay me. Soon after that, I was able to move up and was the first woman manager in my district. I had to knock down my own walls. When I tell this story now, it seems ridiculous to younger women who have never experienced being told that they don't qualify for positions because of their gender.

As women, we do make a difference, but we have to acknowledge that in our journey as leaders we still have a long way to go. Lane gives the great example of how she and the women of her generation had to break down doors by their own initiative at a time when women were limited to specific jobs and many of these jobs were not even in leadership positions. Yet, in spite of the adversities, she and others have maintained their integrity. They did not become resentful, nor did they take it out on others. When their time came to become leaders, they kept their humanity and were able to lead in the most compassionate way.

Disadvantages still exist today for women. Melanie makes a good point that sometimes women in leadership positions are afraid to make unpopular decisions. A real leader has to be able to make a decision on behalf of her people. The stereotype that Lane referred to — women being too soft — is still a reality that women should keep in mind. The ability to make decisions is an important leadership quality, and women should claim it. The women in this book do show, though, that they can make decisions as leaders. Whether or not a decision is popular, these women are able to take action effectively while still being kind.

The advantages that women bring to the workplace are tremendous and outweigh any perceived disadvantage from themselves or others. Jennifer points out that people tend to be more open with women and are able to share. This is great, because ideas are more easily expressed in such an environment, and that is good for everyone. As Alma and Lane share, too, women are more highly developed in terms of intuition. As leaders, women can see the road ahead a little differently than men, and that perspective is invaluable. Women also are better at relationship building, an attribute that is especially valuable when working in teams. As

Melanie and Alma share, women have finely tuned listening skills and are willing to listen. This is a wonderful advantage. If people feel that they are being heard, they feel better about their jobs. Not only that, Elizabeth shares from her research studies in business school that women tend to consider people's feelings more. This is essential to compassionate leadership, and it underscores the importance of people being open to share. She also brings up the point that women think more holistically than men, meaning they may more easily see the bigger picture.

Also, just being a woman can be an advantage. Elizabeth makes the point that since women are still in the minority in business, their perspectives stand out in contrast to those of their male counterparts.

Finally, Elizabeth's story about her mother and Lane's reflection about her past job struggles show us how far women have come in the last few decades. It is difficult to believe that women had to answer strange questions about their menstrual cycle on the job or had to fight against such strange stereotypes that prevented women from even being considered for a job as a cook in a restaurant, let alone a manager. Women are rising up in leadership positions more and more now, and the women in this book are a testament that these days "nice girls" can be on top.

CONCLUSION

Let's face it. Most people want to be nice. When it comes to being a leader, though, being nice is a challenge. The good news is that the women in this book have successfully shown us how we all can do it and get the best results. They have shared their acquired wisdom on so many aspects of compassionate and effective leadership, so that we all will know what to do in any given situation. These women were not *born* leaders; they learned from their experiences and took advantage of opportunities. They also learned from the mentors in their lives; they took those lessons and applied them to the different aspects of their own leadership styles. Then, by way of this book, these women have continued their mentorship role by teaching us all how to be kind, compassionate, wise, and very effective leaders.

The future for women in leadership is bright. Women, more and more, are breaking ground in all aspects of society, taking on high-level leadership positions in business and in politics. Women need not ever feel they must deny their own natural instincts in order to succeed again. They should feel free to be themselves. The very reason, as conveyed in this book, is that female leaders offer a refreshing perspective that inspires and encourages people, like a kind and strong mother who nurtures her children. In the information age we live in, this type of compassionate leadership is vital to inspiring the innovative thinking that will drive our future and our economy into success.

The future is up to you. I ask that you take the lessons given by the wonderful women in this book and make them your own. Take what they have learned and apply it to your own life. You will see that you, too, can lead while presenting the instinctual kind, warm, and compassionate sides of yourself. You will see that leading in this way creates a win-win situation for you as well as those who follow you. Let the women in this book be your mentors, and use their wisdom as your guide. Seek out other mentors so you can continue learning, and, in turn, mentor others. Women will succeed more often when other women lend a helping hand.

I will say it again — the future of women in leadership is bright. It is up to you to make it shine with warmth and compassion!

NOTES

1 Baker, W.F., O'Malley, M. (2008). Leading with Kindness: How Good People Consistently Get Superior Results. New York: *Amacom*

2 Eagly, A.H., Carli, L.L. (2003). The female leadership advantage: an evaluation of the evidence. *The Leadership Quarterly*, 14: 807-834

3 Drucker, P.F. (1999) *Management Challenges for the 21st Century*. New York: HarperCollins

4 Taylor, F.W. (2006). *The Principles of Scientific Management*. Fairfield, IA: 1st World Library Literary Society.

5 Moskowitz, M., Levering, R., Tkaczyk, C. (Feb, 2010) The 100 Best Companies to Work For. *Fortune*, 161:2

6 Terez, Tom (2003). The Power of Nice. *Workforce*, 82: 22-28

7 Hareli, S., Shomrat, N., Biger, N. (2005). The role of emotions in employees' explanations for failure in the workplace. *Journal of Managerial Psychology*, 20: 8: 663-680

8 Bennis, W. (2009; 1989) *On Becoming a Leader*. New York: Basic Books, pp. 85-88

RESOURCES

Baker, W.F., O'Malley, M. (2008). *Leading with Kindness: How Good People Consistently Get Superior Results.* New York: Amacom

Bass, B. M. (1998). *Transformational Leadership: Industry, Military, and Educational Impact.* Mahwah, NJ: Erlbaum.

Bennis, W. (2009; 1989) *On Becoming a Leader.* New York: Basic Books.

Book, E.W. (2000) *Why the Best Man for the Job is a Woman: The Unique Female Qualities of Leadership.* New York: Harper Business

Coughlin, L. (2005) *Enlightened Power: How Women are Transforming the Practice of Leadership.* San Francisco: Jossey-Bass

Drucker, P.F. (1999) *Management Challenges for the 21st Century.* New York: HarperCollins

Eagly, A.H., Carli, L.L. (2003). *The Female Leadership Advantage: An Evaluation of the Evidence.* The Leadership Quarterly, 14: 807-834

Friedman, C., Yorio, K. (2006) *The Girl's Guide to Being a Boss (Without Being a Bitch).* New York: Morgan Road Books

George, W. (2003). *Authentic Leadership: Rediscovering the Secrets to Creating Lasting Value.* San Francisco, CA: Jossey-Bass

Goleman, D., Boyatzis, R., & McKee, A. (2002). *Primal Leadership: Realizing the Power of Emotional Intelligence*. Boston, MA: Harvard Business School Press.

Hareli, S., Shomrat, N., Biger, N. (2005). *The Role of Emotions in Employees' Explanations for Failure in the Workplace.* Journal of Managerial Psychology, 20: 8: 663-680

Hegelson, S. (1990). *The Female Advantage: Women's Ways of Leadership*. New York: Doubleday Currency.

Jackson, R.M. (1998). *Destined for Equality: The Inevitable Rise of Women's Status*. Cambridge, MA: Harvard University Press.

Jarvis, J. (2009). *What Would Google Do?* New York: HarperCollins

Kahl, J., Donelan, T. (2004) *Leading from the Heart: Choosing to Be a Servant Leader.* Westlake, OH: Kahl & Associates.

Moskowitz, M., Levering, R., Tkaczyk, C. (Feb, 2010) *The 100 Best Companies to Work For*. Fortune, 161:2

Rosener, J.B. (1995). *America's Competitive Secret: Utilizing Women as Management Strategy*. New York: Oxford University Press.

Taylor, F.W. (2006). *The Principles of Scientific Management*. Fairfield, IA: 1st World Library Literary Society.

Terez, Tom (2003). *The Power of Nice.* Workforce, 82: 22-28

www.ingramcontent.com/pod-product-compliance
Lightning Source LLC
Chambersburg PA
CBHW070542200326
41519CB00013B/3098